HOW PEC
FAMOUS

HOW PEOPLE BECOME FAMOUS

Geniuses of Self-Marketing from Albert Einstein to Kim Kardashian

Rainer Zitelmann

Management Books 2000

First published in Germany in 2020 as *Die Kunst, berühmt zu werden: Genies der Selbstvermarktung von Albert Einstein bis Kim Kardashian*

Translated by Sebastian Taylor, Capital Language Solutions, Berlin

This English language edition first published in 2021 by Management Books 2000 Ltd
36 Western Road
Oxford OX1 4LG
Tel: 0044 (0) 1865 600738
Email: info@mb2000.com

Web: www.mb2000.com

This English language edition is published by arrangement with Maria Pinto-Peuckmann, Literary Agency, World Copyright Promotion, Kaufering, Germany and Co-Agent Martha Halford-Fumagalli, Martha Halford PR.

British Library Cataloguing in Publication Data is available

ISBN 9781852527891

CONTENTS

INTRODUCTION:

THE GENIUSES OF SELF-MARKETING

People who are ambitious, people who want to achieve something extraordinary in life and are not willing to settle for an average existence, are usually driven by one of three motives: they want money, power or fame. After conducting extensive research and writing several bestsellers on getting rich, I began to take an interest in how people succeed in becoming famous. I started to read and analyze tens of thousands of pages of the life stories of famous people, and it became clearer and clearer to me that remarkable achievements are only one aspect of why someone becomes famous. There is another factor and it is even more important: the ability to market yourself.

At the same time, learning more about the principles of self-marketing is not only important for people who want to become famous. Beliefs such as "quality alone is a guarantee of success" and "modesty is a virtue" prevent so many people from getting on in life. No matter whether you are an entrepreneur, a freelancer or self-employed, if you are not able to showcase what you do in the best light, if you are unable to ensure that the right people hear about your achievements, you will be overtaken by others who know how to market themselves more effectively. If you are an employee, you will soon notice that you are left treading water as colleagues who do know how to beat their own drums effectively are rewarded with promotion after promotion. You may react with bitterness and complain about how unfair the world (or your boss) is. Or you could subject your beliefs to constant self-critical analysis and learn from people who have mastered the art of self-marketing. In this book you will find portraits of twelve individuals who all have one thing in common: they understood the importance of self-marketing better than almost anyone else and were (or are) geniuses in this field.

This introduction is primarily written for impatient readers, who want to learn about the most important aspects of self-marketing as quickly as they can. For the more devoted reader, I recommend starting with the twelve portraits and then coming back to this introduction to consolidate the most important points. So, it's up to you now whether you want to skip the next few pages and jump ahead to the first chapter, or whether you can't wait to learn the most important secrets of self-marketing.

The personalities portrayed in this book could not be more different. Our journey begins with Albert Einstein, the Nobel Prize winner and inventor of the theory of relativity, and ends with Kim Kardashian, whose supposed claim to fame is her curvaceous derrière. And what could possibly connect a giant of the intellectual stage such as Steven Hawking with Muhammad Ali, whose IQ tests were always far below-average, or Princess Diana, whose only notable awards at school were a "Most Popular Girl" trophy and a prize for the best-kept guinea pig?

As different as they are, they are all among the small handful of people on this planet to become absolute masters of the art of self-marketing. One might argue that they became so famous simply because they were the best in their respective fields or, like Diana, particularly likeable. And indeed, many of the figures portrayed in this book have accomplished the extraordinary in their chosen professions. But if you take a closer look, you will see that the scale of their fame often far exceeds their achievements. Take Stephen Hawking, probably the most famous scientist of his time. He was well aware that, "To my colleagues, I'm just another physicist, but to the wider public I became possibly the best-known scientist in the world."[1] An ingenious self-marketer, Hawking enjoyed a far higher profile than many Nobel Prize winners, despite the fact that he never won the Nobel Prize and, to his peers, he was by no means the exceptional scientist the public perceived him to be. For instance, a survey of physicists around the millennium by *Physics World* magazine did not even place him among the top ten most important living physicists.[2]

Donald Trump likes to brag about his achievements as a real estate developer, but many real estate developers in New York have been far more successful than Trump. He has always boasted about his wealth, but year after year the *Forbes* ranking of the richest Americans has concluded that he is nowhere near as rich as he claims to be.

The same cannot be said for Muhammad Ali. Not only was he the most famous athlete of the twentieth century, he was also the undisputed heavyweight champion of the world three times. His achievements in boxing were truly exceptional. But they were not the decisive factor behind his incredible popularity. Muhammad Ali – born Cassius Clay Jr. – was a major celebrity even before his first successful title fight against the reigning heavyweight champion of the world, Sonny Liston, in 1964. A year before his victory, *Time* devoted a full front page to Clay. Having analyzed all of Ali's fights, his biographer, Jonathan Eig, provides an honest assessment: "By all these statistical measures, the man who called himself 'The Greatest' was below average for much of his career."[3]

Arnold Schwarzenegger, the most famous bodybuilder of all time, was without doubt outstandingly talented. He won the ultimate accolade in bodybuilding, the Mr. Olympia title, on an astonishing seven occasions. But other bodybuilders at the time – including Frank Zane – had more harmonious physiques. Experts agree that Schwarzenegger owed his seventh Mr. Olympia title solely to his celebrity status, not his muscle development. And after Schwarzenegger retired his posing briefs, there were bodybuilders with significantly more muscle mass, such as Ronnie Coleman, who became Mr. Olympia eight times. But unless you happen to be a bodybuilding expert, you have probably never even heard of Coleman, whereas pretty much everyone on the planet has heard of Schwarzenegger. Austrian-born Schwarzenegger was tremendously successful in a variety of domains but, above all, he was a brilliant salesman. In his autobiography, he writes: "No matter what you do in life, selling is part of it … But you can do the finest work and if people don't know, you have nothing! In politics it's the same: no matter whether you're working on environmental policy or education or economic growth, the most important thing is to make people aware."[4]

Madonna is a magnificent and extraordinarily successful performing artist. According to *Billboard's* Hot 100 Artists ranking, Madonna is the most successful female solo artist of all time and achieves second place in the overall ranking, just behind The Beatles.[5] And *Time* included her in its "The 25 Most Powerful Women of the 20th Century" list.[6] Yet experts all agree that Madonna's extraordinary success has little to do with outstanding vocal abilities. Camille Barbone, Madonna's mentor and early manager, once observed, "Gifted? No. She was a meat-and-potatoes musician. She had just enough skill to write a song or play guitar."[7] In 1995, Madonna was chosen to play the lead in the film version of the musical *Evita*. Madonna – world-famous and at the height of her career – enlisted an esteemed voice coach to help improve her distinctly average vocal technique.[8]

One of the most famous social media celebrities of the modern age is Kim Kardashian West. She has amassed more than 236 million followers on Instagram, even more than Lionel Messi (233 million), the record winner of the FIFA World Player of the Year Award with six titles since 2009. On Twitter, Kim has 69 million followers, almost as many as former American President Donald Trump had before he was banned (well over 70 million),[9] and more than CNN's breaking news feed (58 million). The well-known American TV presenter Barbara Walters didn't mince her words when she accused Kim of never having done anything particularly special: "You don't really act; you don't sing; you don't dance … You don't have any – forgive me – any talent!"[10] Undeniably, Kim had failed as an actress, singer and dancer. But like few others before or after her, she mastered the art of self-marketing.

Of course, this book does also include individuals who, regardless of their self-marketing skills, have made unique contributions to the course of human history. This small group of exceptional men and women includes, most notably, Albert Einstein, the father of the theory of relativity. But can Einstein's scientific achievements explain his fame? Of course not. Even though he fascinated the general public, newspapers devoted extensive front page coverage to his every move and everyone knew his name, hardly anyone understood his theory. Charlie Chaplin, who often appeared together with Einstein, offered the following explanation: "They cheer me because they all understand me, and they cheer you, because no one understands you."[11] In an interview with a journalist, Einstein once observed: "You ask whether it makes a ludicrous impression on me to observe the excitement of the crowd for my teaching and my theory, of which it, after all, understands nothing? I find it funny and at the same time interesting to observe this game."[12]

What many people don't realize is that Einstein, like all of the distinguished figures in this book, spent a great deal of time and considerable effort marketing himself. His fame did not arrive out of the blue and was certainly no coincidence. And it definitely defies explanation in terms of his scientific achievements as a physicist alone, which, after all, no layman can judge.

So, were these geniuses of self-marketing perhaps only the creations of skillful PR strategists and managers? No. Andy Warhol, for example, was more content to have works of art made by his assistants than he was to delegate what was his core competence: self-marketing. Of course, many of the individuals portrayed here also employed expert PR consultants (including Schwarzenegger and Trump), but these were only advisors; they were not the masters, their prominent clients were. I have therefore decided not to include a number of famous people whose celebrity was largely the creation of their managers and agents – such as Elvis Presley or perhaps Greta Thunberg.

The twelve geniuses of self-marketing featured in this book all knew full well how to grab the limelight and turn themselves into distinctive brands. Like every successful brand, they were instantly recognizable and set themselves apart from their peers. They turned specific features of their appearance into unmistakable trademarks – just like products.

Caricaturists do not have to be particularly skilled artists to draw Donald Trump, Andy Warhol, Arnold Schwarzenegger, Kim Kardashian or Karl Lagerfeld. In the course of his life, Lagerfeld built his public image – the Lagerfeld brand – around a series of distinctive features. He did not establish his brand overnight or with a single conscious decision – he cultivated his celebrity over the years. "I don't put on a costume like Charlie Chaplin. My hairstyle, my sunglasses, they have all come to me over the years. Slowly but surely, I have become like a caricature of myself."[13] As he developed his signature style, a distinctive trademark emerged: the fingerless gloves, the powdered braid, the stand-up collar, the sunglasses and, at times, a fan.

Thanks to his unmistakable hairstyle, Trump certainly makes life easy for caricaturists. His hairstyle reflects his personality: it's certainly not beautiful, but it's unmistakable and eye-catching. "Poke fun if you will, but the painstakingly constructed swoosh and the artificial glow of Trump's coiffure make him instantly recognizable." says his biographer Michael D'Antonio, "Without it, he might stand in front of Trump Tower and escape notice. With it, he is mobbed. His hair has drawing power, even if he didn't set out, in the beginning, to cultivate a billboard atop his head."[14]

Albert Einstein consciously cultivated his image as a disheveled scientist, as an eccentric who attached little to no importance to clothes, detested formal collars and ties, did not comb his long hair, wore no socks and left his shirts open. As his biographer Jürgen Neffe writes, he "fit the cliché of the avant-garde artist of science to a T"[15] and was "the ideal object for photographers and reporters and all other priests of popularity with whom he has lived in a strange symbiosis."[16] Once, when asked about his profession, he replied self-ironically, "fashion model."[17] Rumor has it that as soon as photographers approached, Einstein mussed up his hair with both hands to restore his quintessential image as an eccentric professor.[18]

In 1957, Andy Warhol had cosmetic surgery, a procedure that was still very unusual at the time. He started wearing toupees and sunglasses. Even though he was already earning a substantial amount and was certainly able to buy expensive clothes and luxury items, he reworked new suits and shoes before putting them on, until they looked worn out and fitted the image of the eccentric artist.[19] Warhol wore a black leather jacket, tight black jeans (including pantyhose), T-shirts and high-heeled boots. His wigs were silver-gray, his Factory studio was silver, and this was the color of the Warhol brand. On some occasions, he even used make-up to emphasize his Slavic features and paleness.[20]

Steve Jobs also created unmistakable trademarks around his own image. At his product presentations he wore shorts, sneakers and a black turtleneck sweater. His sweaters were created by the famous designer Issey Miyake and he had about 100 of them made. In a similar way, Schwarzenegger transformed the bicep pose into his trademark. Schwarzenegger had his biceps, Karl Lagerfeld had his braid, sunglasses and stand-up collar, Donald Trump has his hair, Andy Warhol had his wig, Albert Einstein his nutty professor look, and Kim Kardashian has her bottom. When she won the Entrepreneur of the Year award at the Glamour Women of the Year Awards in London in June 2011, interest in her buttocks was so great that they were actually X-rayed to determine whether they were real or contained implants.[21] Kim has always succeeded in attracting attention with spectacular photos that focus on her backside. At one point, even the reputable *Daily Telegraph* reported on one particular image that attracted an enormous amount of attention: "In September 2014 niche title *Paper Magazine* created one of the biggest cultural events of the year, and perhaps the decade, when they set out to 'Break The Internet' with the help of a naked Kim Kardashian. The image of Kim Kardashian balancing a champagne glass on her perfectly-sculpted derriere accompanied by the hashtag #BreakTheInternet sent a sharing shockwave through the web. The site received over 50 million hits in one day, equating to 1 per cent of all internet traffic that day in the US."[22]

One of the cast-iron rules of self-marketing is that you don't need to look *better*, you need to look *different*. Kim Kardashian and Madonna are by no means unattractive, but there are tens of thousands of more beautiful women in America. And Stephen Hawking went one further: he managed to turn his disability into an advantage. When asked how he managed to be so well-known, he replied: "This is partly because scientists, apart from Einstein, are not widely known rock stars, and partly because I fit the stereotype of a disabled genius. I can't disguise myself with a wig and dark glasses – the wheelchair gives me away."[23] As the publication of Hawking's *A Brief History of Time* approached, his publisher understood the marketing value of Hawking's disability and chose a photograph of Hawking in a wheelchair set against a starry sky for the cover that Hawking himself described as "miserable."[24] The book spent 147 weeks on *The New York Times* bestseller list, a record-breaking 237 weeks on the London *Times* bestseller list[25] and has since been translated into 40 languages and sold more than 10 million copies worldwide.

Standing out doesn't necessarily mean being better than everyone else, but it does mean being different. And being different requires provocation, an art that each of the figures portrayed in this book have mastered. Andy Warhol's fame as an artist is founded on his ability to provoke and polarize. In 1964, he was commissioned to make a mural for the U.S. pavilion at the World Expo in New York. The painting was supposed to highlight the United States as the exhibition's host – and Warhol decided to depict the 13 most wanted criminals in the country. In the run up to the Expo, government officials declared that they did not want such images to be used to represent the United States and, two weeks before the opening, Philip Johnson, the pavilion's architect, gave

Warhol 24 hours to remove the offending images. Warhol then made a counterproposal – to replace the portraits of the criminals with 25 portraits of Robert Moses, the president of the World's Fair Corporation. But this proposal was also rejected. Warhol decided to paint over *Thirteen Most Wanted Men* with aluminum paint, which naturally attracted even more attention.

Trump also owes much of his success to his contempt for social norms, his rejection of accepted rules of language, his refusal to recognize taboos and his disdain for political correctness – all of which his followers have found liberating. Although Trump has frequently been caught out by fact-checkers, his followers describe him as honest because he always says what he thinks: "I could give an answer that's perfect and everything's fine and nobody would care about it, nobody would write about it, or I could give an honest answer, which becomes a big story … I think people are tired of politically correct people."[26]

Muhammad Ali was deliberately provocative with his pronouncements and loud bragging, fully convinced that many spectators only attended his fights to see him, a cocky young black man, "get his pretty face disfigured." He embraced the Nation of Islam, an association which – unlike the civil rights movement led by Martin Luther King Jr. – strictly rejected integration and opposed white racism with black racism. He hit the headlines for refusing to be drafted to the military and for his opposition to the war in Vietnam. Ali's most famous statement in declaring himself a conscientious objector was "I ain't got no quarrel with them Viet Cong." This sentence was quoted and printed on T-shirts all over America – it became one of the most frequently cited statements Ali ever made. With these words, Ali aligned himself with the generation of Vietnam War protesters around the world in the 1960s. In 1965, the World Boxing Association and the New York State Athletic Commission suspended Ali's boxing license. Other boxing commissions followed suit and Ali was stripped of his world championship title.[27] In June 1967, he was sentenced to five years in prison for refusing to serve in the United States military, a sentence he never actually had to serve as it was revoked three years later.

Albert Einstein, like many successful self-marketers, also positioned himself as a rebel. Almost everything he did was designed to provoke and he was not prepared to submit to prevailing norms if he deemed them absurd: "He rebelled against any kind of authoritarian structure: against rigid rules in school and at the university; against the dictates of bourgeois life; against conventions such as dress codes; against dogmatism in religion and physics; against militarism, nationalism, and government ideology; and against bosses and employers."[28]

Steve Jobs never spoke like the CEO of a major company. He communicated like a visionary politician or the leader of a revolutionary movement. However, he was not planning on changing the world through politics, but with technology. Jobs described Apple's customers as follows: "The people who buy [Apple computers] do think different. They are the creative spirits in this world, and they're out to change the world. *We* make tools for those kinds of people ... We too are going to think differently and serve the people who have been buying our products from the beginning. Because a lot of people think they're crazy, but in that craziness we see genius."[29]

Madonna realized that provocation and violating social norms is one of the keys to building brand identity. "I'd rather be on people's minds than off," was Madonna's motto.[30] While other public figures are afraid of negative press, Madonna saw – much like Donald Trump – that negative press could actually be positive and expand her fan base. "She believed that the more the press dubbed her style 'trashy,' the more vociferous the parental objection to her look, it would only encourage rebellious children to emulate her ... Her success most certainly validated the blueprint for attention drawn up by Madonna as a child: do something to shock people and, if it's outrageous enough, it will get them talking. She didn't care what they were saying, as long as they were saying *something* about her."[31]

Madonna's public provocations mostly revolved around sex, including the frequent juxtaposition of sex and religion. In the video to one of her most successful songs "Like a Prayer," Madonna kisses a black Christ, is marked with stigmata, has tears of blood streaming down her face and dances in front of a field of burning candles. The video was relegated to late-night MTV and, when church leaders called for their congregations to boycott Pepsi, the soft drink giant swiftly pulled a big-budget TV commercial featuring Madonna.[32]

During her risqué stage shows, Madonna often simulated masturbation on stage and once, during the North American leg of a world tour, Toronto police even threatened to arrest Madonna for obscenity if she went ahead with the show as planned.[33] In Italy, Catholic pressure groups called for a boycott of Madonna's concerts.[34]

The excitement surrounding Madonna reached a climax in October 1992 when the singer published a book of erotic photographs and text branded with the provocative title *Sex*. The book was a showcase for Madonna's erotic fantasies, which were depicted in text and, far more frequently, photographs. In the book, Madonna explained why she was so into anal sex, while extensive photo spreads depicted her having sex with women. Above all, the book was a textual and visual expression of her affinity to S&M practices. Throughout the book, Madonna also appears engaged in scenes of masturbation. The *Observer* branded it "the desperate confection of an aging scandal addict."[35] The public controversy surrounding *Sex* catapulted the book to number 1 on *The New York Times* bestseller list.[36]

And Madonna's career provides yet another valuable insight: Whenever a figure in the public eye is subjected to an escalating stream of criticism, there is always a danger that the provocateur will respond by becoming even more radical and defiant. In Madonna's case, however, her PR genius comes to the fore and she knows precisely when to back down – or better still – to find a way back into her audience's hearts.[37] Following the scandal surrounding her book, Madonna set off on a four-continent world tour, which she called "The Girlie Show." As her biographer J. Randy Taraborrelli observed, "While still sexy, it was more of an innocent burlesque rather than a blatant attempt to shock. Gone were the hardcore S&M images and the blasphemous religious iconology of the previous two years."[38]

Many self-marketers became famous as the result of scandals and offensive or provocative subject matter, before later trying to correct their images. One such figure is Oprah Winfrey, who became popular for her raunchy, tabloid-style talk shows. In prudish America, sleazy subjects equaled high ratings. It's a lesson Oprah learned during her formative years as a talk show host and held to in later years. One show, for instance, was called "The Man with the Micro-Penis." On another occasion, she dedicated a show to "The Thirty-Minute Orgasm."[39] There was no limit to her imagination when it came to sex-related subject matter: men who have been raped; women who have borne children by their own fathers; women abused during pregnancy; female teachers who had sex with schoolboys; a beauty queen who was raped by her husband, etc.[40]

On one occasion she invited nudists onto her show. On another show, she interviewed a woman who had not had a single orgasm during her eighteen-year marriage – together with the male sex surrogate who was giving her orgasm lessons. She interviewed a sex-addicted woman who had slept with 25 men in a single night,[41] as well as three female porn stars, who shared graphic details of male ejaculations.[42]

Later in her career, she attempted to shed this image and declared, "I used to be better sex and perfect orgasm. Then it was diet. The trend of the nineties is family and nurturing."[43] She started to present more shows on topics such as "How to Have a Happy Step Family" and "The Family Dinner Experiment."[44]

She also reflected more critically on the kind of shows she had initially been so successful with and admitted: "I've been guilty of doing trash TV and not even thinking it was trash."[45] Winfrey increasingly shifted her focus to more intellectual topics, and even launched Oprah's Book Club.

Ali is another of the figures in this book who, later in his career, increasingly toned down his political statements. Only rarely did he refer to whites – as he had previously done – as devils. And although he remained loyal to the Nation of Islam's leader, Elijah Muhammad, he did not talk about his devotion quite as often as before.[46] He no longer visited college campuses to speak out against the Vietnam War and stopped making politically inflammatory statements. "He gave the impression of a man who, above all else, was glad to be a boxer again."[47]

Ali even went as far as to publicly retract his earlier statement about having no quarrel with the Viet Cong. Now, he declared that he stood by his decision to oppose the draft, but, "I wouldn't have said that thing about the Viet Cong. I would have handled the draft different. There wasn't any reason to make so many people mad."[48] Ali, a hero to the left-wing students of the 1960s, now irked many of his former supporters with his public shows of support for the Republican presidential candidate, Ronald Reagan, who was an established hate figure among left-wingers.[49] Ali's reconciliation with America was confirmed when he received the Presidential Medal of Freedom, the country's highest civilian honor, from Republican President George W. Bush in 2005.[50]

Without exception, the geniuses of self-marketing portrayed in this book complained that the publicity they courted had a negative side. But they had chosen their paths themselves and the fame they achieved was no coincidence. One key to their fame was the creative PR stunts they used to attract media coverage.

Andy Warhol became famous with his pictures of oversized Campbell's soup cans. When his pictures were exhibited to the public for the first time, lined up along the gallery walls like supermarket displays, Warhol was initially ridiculed. His paintings were art, Warhol claimed, even if they didn't look like it. A rival gallery filled its display windows from top to bottom with Campbell's soup cans, accompanied by the slogan: "The real thing for only 33 cents a can!" Warhol then took a photographer to the nearest supermarket and had a picture taken of him signing "the real thing," namely actual Campbell's soup cans. One of the photos was picked up by the leading news agency Associated Press and distributed halfway around the world.[51]

Hawking always came up with new marketing ideas to draw attention to his scientific theories. Other scientists might have turned their noses up at addressing topics such as time travel – and if they ever did, they would have done so in scientific articles in academic journals. But Hawking had different ideas. On June 28, 2009, he organized a party for time travelers in his college, Gonville & Caius in Cambridge, to show a film about time travel. The room was decorated with balloons and "Welcome, Time Travelers" banners. To make sure that only genuine time travelers would come, he decided to send out invitations after the party and announce it on his 2010 TV show. "On the day of the party, I sat in college hoping, but no one came. I was disappointed, but not surprised, because I had shown that if general relativity is correct and energy density is positive, time travel is not possible. I would have been delighted if one of my assumptions had turned out to be wrong."[52]

On another occasion he made headlines for a scientific wager with the physicist Kip Thorne. They bet on whether or not the Cygnus X-1 system contained a black hole. The wager itself was nothing unusual, but the prize certainly was. If Thorne won their bet, Hawking promised him a year's subscription to the men's magazine *Penthouse*. "In the years following the bet, the evidence for black holes became so strong that I conceded and gave Kip a subscription to *Penthouse*, much to the displeasure of his wife."[53]

Muhammad Ali's ingenuity when it came to getting himself into newspapers and magazines was equally impressive. His spontaneous creativity is perfectly illustrated by the time, early in his career, when he tricked the world into believing that he regularly trained underwater. In 1961, *Sports Illustrated* assigned a photographer, Flip Schulke, to take pictures of Clay. At one point, Clay asked Schulke which other magazines he worked for. Clay was excited to hear that the photographer's pictures regularly appeared in *Life*, the highest circulation magazine in the United States at that time. Clay asked Schulke if he would photograph him for *Life*, but the photographer explained that he worked on assignment and would have to pitch the idea to his editors, who would most likely turn it down – this was, after all, still very early in Clay's career. But Clay didn't let up and asked Schulke about his other work. When the photographer revealed that he specialized in underwater photography, Clay told him a "secret": "I never told nobody this, but me and Angelo have a secret. Do you know why I'm the fastest heavyweight in the world? I'm the only heavyweight that trains underwater." Clay claimed that he worked out underwater for the same reason other athletes wear heavy shoes when they train. "Well, I get in the water up to my neck and I punch in the water, and when I get out of the water I'm lightning fast because there's no resistance."[54] Schulke was suspicious at first, but Clay offered to let Schulke attend and take pictures of one of his underwater training sessions exclusively for *Life*. Schulke pitched Clay's proposal to *Life*, who liked the idea of running an article on Clay's unconventional underwater training routine. Of course, Clay had made up the entire story, but the successful outcome of his tall tale, namely a portrait in the highest circulation magazine in the United States, confirmed the effectiveness of this approach.

Even as a teenager, Arnold Schwarzenegger had an extraordinarily keen sense for unusual methods of self-marketing. One icy cold day in November, Schwarzenegger took a stroll along a shopping street in Munich wearing only his posing briefs. His mentor, Albert Busek, called a few editors he knew and asked them, "You remember Schwarzenegger, who won the stone-lifting contest? Well, now he's Mr. Universe and he's at Stachus square in his underwear."[55] The next day, his picture was in the newspaper. Schwarzenegger was depicted standing in his posing briefs on a construction site, flanked by a huddle of construction workers looking on in utter amazement.

During the presidency of George H. W. Bush, Schwarzenegger was appointed as the government's "fitness czar." If anything, his new role was nothing special. The president already had several czars who were supposed to champion different issues, but none of them had managed to attract much attention. Here, however, is where Schwarzenegger's PR genius once again comes into play. "My own mission," he explained to President Bush, "should be to get out and promote." Bush was surprised that Schwarzenegger wanted to travel to all 50 states to carry out his duties as fitness czar. "I love being on the road and meeting people and selling. That's what I do best."[56] Normally, the White House press office would have sent out a short press release to announce the president's new "fitness czar," and that would have been buried under the pile of many other reports landing in newsrooms across the country. Schwarzenegger, however, suggested to Bush that the announcement should take place in the Oval Office. That, Schwarzenegger explained, would give the press an opportunity to take photographs and should be followed by a press conference where Schwarzenegger could clarify his new role and the President could explain why Schwarzenegger was exactly the right man for the job.[57]

The art of successful public relations is all about formulating specific, memorable soundbites to communicate core messages and getting the media to do much of your marketing work for you and "frame" events in the way you want them to. Steve Jobs was an absolute master at creating short, captivating headlines, as was Princess Diana. Her greatest PR coup was a TV interview about her failed marriage to Prince Charles. She had spent weeks practicing her lines and the interview was finally broadcast on November 14, 1995. On the night of the broadcast, the streets of London were deserted. Twenty-three million British viewers sat transfixed in front of their television sets[58] – and what they saw was a carefully crafted performance that hit all the right notes. Like a PR script, she had developed certain core messages that did not fail to have the desired effect:

- "I'd like to be the queen of people's hearts …"
- "There were three of us in the marriage …" (a reference to Camilla Parker Bowles)

- "The Establishment that I married into – they have decided that I'm a non-starter ..."[59]
- (About the motives of her opponents): "I think it was out of fear, because here was a strong woman doing her bit, and where was she getting her strength from to continue?"[60]

She told her story in a way that every wronged woman could identify with. Asked about her own affair with James Hewitt, she avoided admitting to a sexual relationship, deftly brushed aside the question of a physical relationship and shifted to the emotional, saying, "Yes, I adored him. Yes, I was in love with him. But I was very let down."[61] The public responded as she knew they would. She won their support by making it easy for them to identify with her struggles and her complaints about the "Establishment" that had "decided" she was a failure. And although she was by no means a feminist, she tapped into the feminist zeitgeist by framing any criticism of her as resistance to an independent and strong woman "who was doing her bit" in her very own way. Diana's core messages had their desired effect. On the Wednesday after the interview aired, a survey by the *Daily Mirror* showed 92 percent approval for Diana's television appearance.

These geniuses of self-marketing also realized just how important it is to make the kind of unconventional statements that news outlets will be hungry to quote. In the film "Pumping Iron," Arnold Schwarzenegger compared pumping up his muscles during training with an orgasm: "Blood is rushing into your muscles, that's what we call the pump. Your muscles get a really tight feeling, like you're going to explode ... It's as satisfying to me as coming is; you know, as having sex with a woman and coming."[62] He later explained, "To sell something on TV and stand out, I knew I'd have to do something spectacular, so I came up with comments like pumping up the muscles is much better than having sex."[63]

When it comes to interviews, the individuals portrayed in this book adopted strategies that were very different from the typical approaches prominent figures use when dealing with journalists' questions. Andy Warhol, for example, was a very difficult interviewee, which actually made him a far more interesting interlocutor. He made a habit of refusing to answer questions, sometimes by simply repeating the question back to his interviewer as his "answer." Not infrequently he switched roles and began to interview his interviewer. His answers often made no sense, but it was precisely this unusual, enigmatic and surprising aspect that made him such a sought-after interviewee for media outlets up and down the country. Warhol often answered questions with a simple "I don't know." Here are just a few examples:

"What is Pop Art trying to say?" – "I don't know."

"How did you get started making movies?" "Uh… I don't know…"

"What is your role, your function in directing a Warhol film?" "I don't know. I'm trying to figure it out."[64]

Warhol turned his habit of giving unexpected, crazy and provocative answers in interviews into one of his most distinct trademarks. For a 1970s art anthology, renowned artists were asked for their thoughts on other well-known artists. When Warhol was asked about the significance of the abstract expressionist Barnett Newman, he answered, "The only way I knew Barney was I think Barney went to more parties than I did."[65] And when asked for his opinion of Pablo Picasso, he said, "Ah, the only thing I can really relate to is his daughter Paloma … I'm just glad he had a wonderful daughter like Paloma."[66]

Einstein was also well-known for surprising reporters with unconventional responses to their questions. When a reporter from *The New York Times* asked Einstein for a comment on his book, he curtly replied: "What I have to say about this book can be found inside the book."[67] Donald Trump makes deliberately provocative statements because he knows they guarantee media attention. "One thing I've learned about the press," explains Trump, "is that they're always hungry for a good story, and the more sensational the better … The point is that if you are a little different, or a little outrageous, or if you do things that are bold or controversial, the press is going to write about you. I've always done things a little differently, I don't mind controversy, and my deals tend to be somewhat ambitious."[68]

It is striking that these geniuses of self-marketing are the sources of so many aphorisms, adages and short verses. The pithy wisdoms of Karl Lagerfeld often struck a chord and became familiar well beyond the world of fashion. Almost everyone will have heard his frequently quoted maxims, which included cutting observations such as, "If you wear sweatpants, you have lost control of your life." From the intellectual giant Albert Einstein to the boxing legend Muhammad Ali, who had difficulty reading and writing, many of these figures published poems and short verses to draw attention to themselves.

One of Ali's most famous PR stunts was predicting the exact round in which his opponents would fall to the canvas. No boxer before him had ever done this and it created great suspense for journalists and audiences alike. Early in his career, Ali also began to compose short verses, which would later become his trademark. For instance, he told a reporter:

"This guy must be done,
I'll stop him in one."[69]

Critics were offended by the fact that Ali would sometimes coast for a full round just to fulfill his prediction. Ali, however, "liked his new gimmick, liked the extra attention that came with his increasingly bold behavior, and he was convinced that publicity would help him get a quicker shot at the championship."[70] He became even more of a showman and turned predicting when his opponents would crash to the canvas into his USP: "I'm not the greatest. I'm the double greatest. Not only do I knock 'em out, I pick the round. I'm the boldest, the prettiest, the most superior, most scientific, most skillfullest fighter in the ring today. I'm the only fighter who goes from corner to corner and club to club debating with fans. I've received more publicity than any fighter in history. I talk to reporters till their fingers are sore."[71]

Geniuses of self-marketing, as the example of Ali confirms, are not only very sure of themselves, they are also entirely uninhibited when it comes to sharing this with the world. We have all become very familiar with Trump's boastful pronouncements. No one could be left in any doubt that he regards himself as the greatest in almost every field: "Sorry losers and haters, but my IQ is one of the highest – and you all know it! Please don't feel so stupid or insecure, it's not your fault."[72]

Oprah Winfrey's self-congratulatory proclamations rival even Muhammad Ali or Donald Trump. For example, in one interview she explained, "I'm very strong ... very strong. I know there is nothing you or anybody can tell me that I don't already know. I have this inner spirit that directs and guides me ... I really like me, I really do. I'd like to know me, if I weren't me."[73] Lagerfeld once greeted a journalist sympathetically with the remark, "I was once a mere mortal like you."[74]

None of the figures in this book ever wanted to be mere mortals like everyone else. They believed they were special from the very beginning.

One of Steve Jobs' closest employees once reported, "He thinks there are a few people who are special – people like Einstein and Ghandi and the gurus he met in India – and he's one of them." On one occasion, Jobs even hinted that he was enlightened.[75]

The fact that the figures you are about to meet in this book became so prominent was by no means a coincidence, and it was certainly no unintended side effect of their other achievements. Each had an overpowering desire to become famous. Madonna's friend Erica Bell remembers a conversation they had about what Madonna most wanted from life. "I want to be famous," was Madonna's instant response, "I want attention." When her friend said she was already getting a lot of attention, Madonna replied, "It's not enough. I want all of the attention in the world. I want everybody in the world to not only know me, but to love me, *love me, love me*."[76] In 2000, at a time when she was already incredibly famous, she admitted, "I have the same goal I've had since I was a little girl. I want to rule the world."[77] On another occasion, she confessed, "I won't be happy until I'm as famous as God."[78]

All of the figures in this book constantly and consciously sought the company of other celebrities because they knew full well this would propel them to an even higher level of fame. Albert Einstein had his picture taken with Charlie Chaplin, Arnold Schwarzenegger married into the Kennedy clan and Kim Kardashian married Kanye West, one of the leading hip hop and pop musicians in the world. In recognition of his impact on popular culture, *Time* magazine featured West in its lists of the 100 most influential people in the world for the first time in 2005 and then again in 2015.

Warhol was desperate to become famous. The subject of fame and celebrity occupied him like no other. He became "synonymous with the culture of celebrity-for-its-own-sake," as one of his biographers wrote.[79] Even as a child, he had an insatiable appetite for movie magazines. He collected "personalized" autographed photographs of film stars.[80] This created a self-perpetuating spiral. He systematically sought out the company of famous people and his rising fame made it increasingly easy for him to meet celebrities, which in turn increased his own fame.[81] As did accepting commissions from famous people, such as the time he worked for the record company of his friend Mick Jagger of the Rolling Stones. It was Warhol who designed the unusual cover for the album Sticky Fingers with the picture of a pair of jeans on the front and back and a zipper that could be pulled down to reveal a tantalizing glimpse of white underwear beneath. "With virtuosity, Warhol took advantage of the celebrity status of his friends and clients for his own publicity and again proved his impressive talent for self-marketing."[82] He increasingly moved in celebrity circles, in a glamorous whirl of movie stars, politicians, fashion czars, famous musicians and celebrities of all stripes. He socialized with Liz Taylor, Jackie Onassis, Shirley MacLaine, Paloma Picasso, Henry Kissinger, Jimmy Carter, Yves Saint Laurent, Diana Ross, Pierre Cardin and John Lennon.[83]

Every one of these geniuses of self-marketing also earned a great deal of money. Although they didn't all become anywhere near as rich as Oprah Winfrey, the world's first black self-made billionaire, they did all earn far more than their peers. Even Einstein and Hawking, who of course did not become nearly as wealthy as Steve Jobs, Madonna or Karl Lagerfeld, managed to earn far more than other leading physicists.

Despite their incredible wealth and celebrity, they always maintained an image of being close to the people – and in many ways they were. The editor of one of Trump's books recalled that, "Trump had this urge to be a really big name, so he cultivated celebrity. But his lifestyle was surprisingly unglamorous … He was not a big New York socialite, never was. He basically enjoyed going upstairs and watching the tube. What he was interested in was celebrity and his businesses – construction, real estate, gambling, wrestling, boxing."[84] In many respects, Trump's lifestyle and interests mean he has far more in common with regular Americans than he does with members of the educated elite. He'd much rather watch boxing, wrestling and reality TV than immerse himself in high culture, read a book or go to the theater. Many working-class Americans want to stay true to their roots; they just want to do so with a lot more money. And this is exactly what Trump embodies, this billionaire who speaks their language and loves the same things they do – quite unlike the intellectuals who regard themselves so highly because they read sophisticated literature or are interested in the arts. Trump has no interest in the subjects intellectuals obsess over. Conversely, he knows a huge amount about pop culture.

Just like Donald Trump, Oprah Winfrey, despite her incredible fortune and fame, has always managed to create the impression that she not only has an affinity for ordinary people and their problems, but that she was in fact one of them.[85] And to a certain extent this is true. The problems Oprah had in her private life – especially her weight and diet issues, but also in her relationships – were the same problems so many of her viewers were also grappling with.

And even Lagerfeld, who so often seemed aloof and arrogant, with the air of a nobleman from centuries gone by, struck the right balance between creating exclusive fashion and designing a collection and perfume for the Swedish mass-marker fashion chain H&M. He combined an air of elitism with egalitarian values: "The upper ten thousand have always been the victims of their own snobbery. Only the most expensive is good enough for them. But it is important not to look down on the 'masses.' We need to offer affordable options. You can still look chic while buying cheap."[86] Stephen Hawking also had no problems with appearing on popular television shows and, to the amazement of many of his colleagues, he actually liked giving interviews to tabloid newspapers. At one point, while looking for a new publisher for a book, one of his non-negotiable conditions was that the book should be available in airport bookstores all across America.

Perhaps one of the reasons these self-marketing geniuses remained so relatable despite their pronounced narcissism and extreme self-centeredness was that they retained a certain sense of self-irony and were able to laugh at themselves – or at least pretend to. Lagerfeld claimed that he was always the first to laugh at himself and was convinced of the therapeutic benefits of not taking yourself too seriously: "Everyone can be grotesque in certain situations. If you pay attention, you'll notice it, too. As long as you are honest with yourself."[87]

According to the people who knew them best, many of the individuals portrayed in this book never really grew up. It has been said that, in certain respects, Albert Einstein, Steve Jobs, Madonna, Andy Warhol and Muhammad Ali remained like children well into their adult lives. They all had a tremendous desire to be free. They wanted to live their lives without limits and were not prepared to conform to social norms. The German news magazine *Der Spiegel* described Lagerfeld as the "pioneer of an age in which staging and image are everything. Radical, free and unique."[88] The same could easily be said of Steve Jobs, Andy Warhol or Arnold Schwarzenegger.

I'd rather not reveal any more of the secrets of these geniuses of self-marketing at this point. Read on for yourself and discover what it was that made these people so famous. I have intentionally chosen not to reveal some of their greatest secrets in this introduction. As you read on through the next twelve chapters, you might want to write them down for yourself. If you too want to become famous, you can certainly learn a lot from these exceptional personalities although you shouldn't try to copy them.

I have organized the individual portraits by their subjects' dates of birth, from Albert Einstein, who was born in 1879, all the way through to Kim Kardashian, who was born 101 years later. Perhaps it is a coincidence, although probably not, but this book begins with a man whose achievements in his field (physics) were greater than any of the other people presented here. And it ends with Kim Kardashian, a woman who has mastered the art of self-marketing to such an extent that she has created an entirely new paradigm in which fame is in no way related to conventional measures of achievement.

CHAPTER ONE

ALBERT EINSTEIN: THE MAN WHO STUCK HIS TONGUE OUT AT THE WORLD

(Granger Historical Picture Archive / Alamy Stock Photo)

Einstein's biographer **Jürgen Neffe** described the physicist as the "first global pop star of science."[89] Albert Einstein's popular image "is better known than that of any other human being."[90] Today, his name is synonymous with "genius." Whenever we refer to someone as an "Einstein," we use it as shorthand to signal their unsurpassable intelligence. But the genius of this physicist was not only that he formulated the theory of relativity, but also that he mastered the art of self-marketing more than any other scientist of his era.

Most scientists address their work exclusively or predominantly at other scientists. They speak at scientific conferences and publish in scientific journals. Any scientist who succeeds in reaching a wider audience knows they could inspire envy among their colleagues and peers within the scientific community. And if they ever dare to write in an easily accessible and understandable way, this is disparagingly dismissed as "popular science." This was precisely what happened with Einstein, who attracted the envy of his colleagues, "not one of [whom] had ever been celebrated like that."[91]

In most cases, scientists dedicate their lives to subject matter so complicated that most laymen cannot even begin to understand what their work is about. This was no different with Einstein. Although he delighted the masses, newspapers featured him on their front pages and he was the talk of the town, hardly anyone could hope to grasp the intricacies of his revolutionary theories. Charlie Chaplin, who frequently appeared in public with Einstein (both thereby employing one of the tools of self-marketing), offered the following explanation: "People cheer me because they all understand me, and they cheer you because nobody understands you."[92]

In an interview with *The New York Times*, Einstein once asked himself, "Why is it that nobody understands me, yet everybody likes me?"[93] In an interview with another journalist, he provided the answer: "You ask whether it makes a ludicrous impression on me to observe the excitement of the crowd for my teaching and my theory, of which it, after all, understands nothing? I find it funny and at the same time interesting to observe this game. I believe quite positively that it is the mysteriousness of what they cannot conceive which places them under a magic spell."[94] As Einstein's biographer Walter Isaacson astutely observed, "The theory had the wondrous mix of *Huh?* and *Wow!* that can capture the public imagination."[95] Einstein appreciated the funny side and even remarked that every cab driver and waiter was busy arguing about whether or not his relativity theory was correct.[96]

On his 50th birthday in 1929, the Berlin correspondent of the *New York Herald Tribune* cabled the entire manuscript of Einstein's latest scientific work to the editorial office, which published it in full.[97] The newspaper's readers would have found it impossible to understand the content of even a single paragraph, but this was precisely what made it so fascinating. For most people, the fact that they did not understand what Einstein said and wrote confirmed more than ever before that he must be one of the greatest geniuses of all times.

The physicist was amused by his popularity and in one of his trademark verses even asked whether it was he or his admirers who could really be "crazy":[98]

"Wherever I go and wherever I stay,
There's always a picture of me on display,
On top of the desk, or out in the hall,
Tied around a neck, or hung on a wall.

Women and men, they play a strange game,
Asking, beseeching: 'Please sign your name.'
From the erudite fellow they brook not a quibble
But firmly insist on a piece of his scribble.

Sometimes, surrounded by all this good cheer,
I'm puzzled by some of the things that I hear,
And wonder, for a moment, my mind not hazy,
If I and not they could really be crazy?"

The cult of Einstein began in November 1919, precisely 14 years after he published his work on "special relativity" and four years after he completed his work on "general relativity." What had previously existed only as a theory was first confirmed by scientific measurements on May 29, 1919 when Sir Arthur Eddington measured the deflection of light during a solar eclipse, empirically confirming Einstein's theory. On November 6, the results were announced at a joint meeting of the Royal Society and the Royal Astronomical Society in London. "At this moment," explained Einstein's biographer Jürgen Neffe, "Albert Einstein was reborn as legend and myth, idol and an icon of an entire era."[99]

But on its own, Einstein's scientific discovery, which was first reported to a wider audience by *The Times* in London on November 7, 1919, does not explain the cult that developed around him over the next few years. And it wasn't just the media chasing stories that made Einstein famous. He pursued a more active public relations strategy than probably any other scientist before him. And he proved to be a master of "using the media for his own ends, just as the media used him for theirs. He was initially rather clumsy in handling the press, but he grew more and more skillful ... His poise in dealing with the press, radio, and film industry enabled him to create something that advertisers might now call a trademark."[100]

In this context, it is important to know the story behind what became the most famous photograph of Einstein ever taken – of him sticking his tongue out at the world. It became his trademark and a pop motif for posters, buttons and T-shirts. It was taken on Einstein's 72nd birthday. In the original image, Einstein is sandwiched between two other people. The conscious effort Einstein put into his own marketing is demonstrated by the fact that he had the photograph cropped so that it only showed his head and had many copies made, which he sent to friends, acquaintances and colleagues.[101]

Isaacson asked, "If he did not have that electrified halo of hair and those piercing eyes, would he still have become science's preeminent poster boy?"[102] Would he have become a cult figure had he looked like his fellow German physicists Max Planck or Niels Bohr? Yet Einstein's appearance was no accident, it was the result of an ingenious self-marketing strategy.

Einstein deliberately cultivated the image of a scientist who couldn't care less about clothing, hated collars and ties, did not comb his long, fuzzy hair, did not wear socks and left his shirts unbuttoned. As his biographer Neffe wrote, he "fit the cliché of the avant-garde artist of science to a T"[103] and was "the ideal object for photographers and reporters and all other priests of popularity with whom he has lived in a strange symbiosis."[104] Once, when asked about his profession, he quipped, "fashion model."[105] Rumor has it that as soon as photographers approached, Einstein mussed up his hair with both hands to restore his quintessential image as an eccentric professor.[106]

On one occasion, Einstein visited the Grand Canyon and spent some time with the chief of a Hopi tribe, who humorously named Einstein the "Great Relative" to reflect the scientist's twin roles as an honorary member of the tribe and as the father of the theory of relativity. "Einstein agreed to pose in a feather headdress. Fodder for the photographers' cameras, but he did not have to be prodded."[107] Einstein did everything he could to cultivate his public image and attract attention. While other scientists share their advances at specialist scientific conferences, Einstein gave lectures to mass audiences worldwide. "Like a founder of a religion," wrote Neffe, "on a mission to preach his doctrine and to gather devotees,

Einstein gave lectures throughout the world in auditoriums filled to overflowing."[108] He was so successful that the German Foreign Office in Berlin even started a file marked "Lectures by Professor Einstein Abroad."[109]

For example, in reference to one of Einstein's trips to Japan, the German ambassador declared, "His trip in Japan was like a triumphal procession." According to the ambassador, "the entire population of Japan, from the highest dignitary to the rickshaw driver, took part, spontaneously, without preparation and affectation!"[110] Einstein's lectures lasted up to five hours. Nevertheless, "Everyone wanted to at least shake hands with the most famous man of the era," reported the ambassador. "The press was full of Einstein stories, both true and false ... There were also caricatures of Einstein, which featured his short pipe and his thick, unruly hair and hinted at the occasional inappropriateness of his clothing."[111]

The *Berliner Tageblatt* reported effusively on one of his visits to the French capital: "This German conquered Paris. All the newspapers printed a picture of him, and an entire literature on Einstein emerged ... Einstein is all the rage. Academics, politicians, artists, rednecks, policemen, cabdrivers, waiters, and pickpockets know when Einstein is giving his lectures. The cocottes in the Café des Paris are asking their dandies whether Einstein wears glasses or is chic. All of Paris knows all about him, and anything Parisians don't know for a fact, they say anyway."[112]

Perhaps more than anywhere else in the world, it was the Americans who followed Einstein's every move and every word with boundless enthusiasm. In New York City, crowds lined the streets and stretched out their hands to touch him, he was celebrated like a sports idol or a movie star.[113] Einstein's visits to America inspired the same kind of hysteria that would greet the Beatles decades later in the swinging 60s. There were girls screeching "Einstein ... Einstein!" as if they wanted to tear the professor's clothes off. Hundreds of excited young women gathered to welcome him with trumpets, rattles, songs, cheerleaders and anything else they could think of. Everywhere he went, reporters chased him through the city, "One of them handed him a paper with formulas and peered at him as though he were an exotic animal who might take the bait, or an extraterrestrial who would react in some bizarre way."[114]

In one conversation with Adolph Ochs, the owner of *The New York Times*, Einstein explained that he regarded the public's interest in him as "psycho-pathological."[115] But he enjoyed the hype and made a point of telling friends how happy he was after a visit to a supermarket, where his admirers obviously didn't get too close to him: "Everyone recognizes me on the street and grins at me."[116] On other occasions, however, he implied that the hysteria was too much for him – and it probably was. In one of his signature verses, he expressed it this way:

> *"A thousand letters in the mail*
> *And every journal tells his tale*
> *What's he to do when in this mood?*
> *He sits and hopes for solitude."*[117]

Einstein was inundated with fan mail and letters from eccentrics, do-gooders and conspiracy theorists. One of them wrote, "My brother, who is sixteen, refuses to get haircuts. He is an admirer of yours and replies to urging that maybe he will grow up to be an Einstein." Another explained, "I must speak to you alone. I am the successor to Jesus Christ. Please hurry." Yet another entreated, "Please inform me whether it is necessary to study physics to prolong life."[118]

The press sometimes ran stories designed to increase the mystique and create new legends around Einstein and his work. On one occasion, *The New York Times* claimed that Einstein came up with his theory of relativity when he saw a man fall from the roof of a neighboring building. Thus, the story created an analogy between Einstein and Sir Isaac Newton: "Inspired as Newton was, but by the fall of a man from a roof instead of the fall of an apple."[119] But Einstein wasn't bothered. As he wrote to a friend, he understood, and accepted, how journalism worked. This kind of exaggeration, he explained, simply satisfies certain needs among the newspaper-reading public.[120]

Nevertheless, Einstein didn't simply attract publicity, he actively sought it. As his biographer Walter Isaacson explained, "Einstein's aversion to publicity, however, existed a bit more in theory than in reality. It would have been possible, indeed easy, for him to have shunned all interviews, pronouncements, pictures, and public appearances. Those who truly dislike the public spotlight do not turn up, as the Einsteins eventually would, with Charlie Chaplin on a red carpet at one of his movie premieres."[121] And the essayist C.P. Snow, after getting to know Einstein personally, observed that he enjoyed the photographers and the crowds. "He had an element of the exhibitionist and the ham. If there had not been that element, there would have been no photographers and no crowds. Nothing is easier to avoid than publicity. If one genuinely doesn't want it, one doesn't get it."[122]

As a genius of self-marketing, Einstein had extraordinary abilities. As the physicist Freeman Dyson noted, "Scientists who become icons must not only be geniuses but also performers, playing to the crowd and enjoying public acclaim."[123] And it is important to remember that at that time, roughly a century ago, serious people – especially those in the realm of science – were appalled by publicity and disdained anyone who actively sought it.

Einstein's friends and colleagues repeatedly reproached him and urged him to exercise more restraint – but he mostly ignored their suggestions. When an acquaintance of Einstein, a writer of humorous and satirical stories, announced that he wanted to publish a book based on conversations with the physicist, one of Einstein's closest friends warned him that he should immediately block the publication of the book because the press would exploit it to strengthen their allegations against him as "a self-promoting Jew."[124] The friend accused Einstein of behaving like a child and taking advice from the wrong people (such as his wife) when it came to such matters.[125]

Einstein justified his penchant for self-promotion by explaining that although the cult of individual personalities is always unjustified, in his case there was a positive aspect because, in a materialistic age, it is a welcome development when people make heroes of men and women whose ambitions lie wholly in the intellectual and moral sphere.[126]

Einstein's obsession with self-promotion led to a serious conflict with Abraham Flexner, founder of the Institute for Advanced Study at Princeton University in the United States. It was Flexner who had invited Einstein, an immigrant to America after Hitler's rise to power, to come to Princeton. Annoyed by Einstein's perceived hunger for publicity, Flexner wrote a sharp letter to Einstein's wife: "This is exactly the sort of thing that seems to me absolutely unworthy of Professor Einstein. It will hurt him in the esteem of his colleagues, for they will believe that he seeks such publicity, and I do not see how they can be convinced that such is not the case."[127]

Flexner was also worried that Einstein's behavior could promote anti-Semitic resentment. After all, the anti-Semitic stereotype regards self-marketing and self-promotion as typical Jewish characteristics. Flexner had invited Einstein to Princeton to conduct his research in peace and quiet and was intensely irritated that his guest continued to seek publicity and attend social and political events. Flexner went as far as to write an official letter to the President of the United States, in which he stressed, "I felt myself compelled this afternoon to explain to your secretary, that Professor Einstein had come to Princeton for the purpose of carrying out his scientific work in seclusion and that it was absolutely impossible to make any exception which would inevitably bring him into public notice."[128]

Flexner even issued an order – without informing Einstein – that all future invitations must go through Flexner. When Einstein found out, he was infuriated and wrote a five-page missive to his friend Rabbi Stephen Wise, on which he wrote as his return address, "Concentration Camp, Princeton."[129]

Albert Einstein, like many successful self-marketers, also positioned himself as a rebel. Almost everything he did was designed to provoke and he was not prepared to submit to prevailing norms if he deemed them absurd: "He rebelled against any kind of authoritarian structure: against rigid rules in school and at the university; against the dictates of bourgeois life; against conventions such as dress codes; against dogmatism in religion and physics; against militarism, nationalism, and government ideology; and against bosses and employers."[130]

An important instrument in Einstein's self-promotion strategy was the hundreds of aphorisms and verses he came up with, many of which are still frequently quoted today. The German poet Theodor Fontane once said that "A good aphorism contains the wisdom of an entire book in one sentence." Einstein was a true master of the aphorism. He formulated pithy, illuminating sentences with apt, surprising and witty turns of phrase to express his view of the world.

Here are just a few examples of his observations on a range of issues:

"Whoever is careless with truth in small matters cannot be trusted in important affairs."[131]

"All of science is nothing more than the refinement of everyday thinking."[132]

"Children don't heed the life experiences of their parents, and nations ignore history. Bad lessons always have to be learned anew."[133]

"Marriage is the unsuccessful attempt to make something lasting out of an incident."[134]

On the subject of psychoanalysis: "I should very much like to remain in the darkness of not having been analyzed."[135]

And, when a reporter from *The New York Times* asked Einstein for a comment on one of his books, he curtly replied: "What I have to say about this book can be found inside the book."[136]

Einstein was also incredibly self-confident. "He was a God, and he knew it," remarked his friend and doctor Gustav Bucky.[137] Einstein had a strong positive self-image even before his great scientific achievements. He had the chutzpah to send a private copy of an early scientific paper to a renowned physicist and wrote to another well-known scientist to "draw his attention to his mistakes."[138] These were both serious violations of basic etiquette that no recent graduate would normally commit. During his first attempt to complete his doctorate, he fell out with his professor.[139] He developed his "special theory of relativity" more or less in his spare time. Given the difficulties he was having getting his foot on the academic ladder, he had no choice but take a job with the patent office, where he worked 48 hours per week.[140]

Many Einstein experts have stressed that – emotionally speaking – he never really grew up. Howard Gardner, professor of psychology at Harvard, described Einstein as "the perpetual child," while the German-American psychoanalyst Erik Erikson reached the same conclusion as Gardner and called Einstein "the victorious child."[141] His biographer Neffe believed that Einstein retained something of his childlike nature for the rest of his life – a trait he shares with other masters of self-promotion portrayed in this book, such as Steve Jobs, Muhammad Ali and Donald Trump.

During the course of his life, Einstein became increasingly involved in politics. Above all, he was a committed pacifist and Zionist. But even as a political activist, he reveled in swimming against the prevailing currents of mainstream opinion and enjoyed provoking people with his controversial views. Was political activism part of his self-marketing strategy or was self-marketing only a means to an end, in order to gain attention for his real-world concerns?

As far as his scientific findings are concerned, Einstein must have recognized – indeed he did recognize – that despite his countless lectures and interviews, he would never be able to explain the ramifications of his theories to non-scientists. People sometimes had completely absurd ideas about Einstein's "theory of relativity." Many mistakenly associated it with entirely unrelated things. It certainly wasn't unusual for people to have heard the term "theory of relativity" and know nothing else about it. The theory, which hardly anyone understood, was disputed by some, while others celebrated it as a new doctrine of salvation, exploiting it for their own means and hailing it as confirmation of their own political and philosophical ideologies and theories. Einstein was too clever not to realize that it would have been hopeless to explain the content of his theory to broad sections of the population. Thus, it is unlikely that his self-marketing strategy was primarily designed to shed light on his scientific findings.

But what about his controversial political statements? It would be an injustice to Einstein to interpret these primarily as tools to attract even greater publicity. In particular, peace, "social justice" and the Zionist cause were issues sincerely close to Einstein's heart. Nevertheless, his political activism also served to further sharpen his brand image and raise his public profile. Conversely, Einstein's public image helped to spread his political messages. So, the two were mutually beneficial: Einstein's self-marketing and his political mission.

Tools Albert Einstein used to build his brand:

1. Lectures and appearances around the world: Einstein traveled to countless countries and gave lectures on his scientific theories and political topics.

2. Active media relations: Einstein cultivated very close relationships with media representatives and journalists and exploited these for his public relations and self-marketing. "Just as the man in the fairy

tale who turned whatever he touched into gold, with me everything is turned into newspaper clamor," he once wrote to his friend Max Born.[142]

3. Provocation and violation of societal norms: Einstein liked to provoke outrage with offbeat views and swam against the current of mainstream opinion. This attracted a great deal of attention.

4. Building a brand image around his idiosyncratic look, which Einstein nurtured to fit the cliché of the nutty but brilliant professor. This included, for example, his long, unkempt hair and deliberately careless clothing (he usually went without socks, for example).

5. Photographs: Einstein jokingly called himself a "fashion model." He deliberately used the impact of unconventional photographs to build his brand. One well-known example is the picture taken of Einstein sticking his tongue out, which he sent to friends and acquaintances because it perfectly encapsulated his role as a provocateur.

6. Aphorisms: The aphorisms and verses he wrote were an important component of his communication with the world at large. These were picked up by the media and were a key plank of his self-marketing strategy.

CHAPTER TWO

ANDY WARHOL:

FROM A SOUP CAN TO GLOBAL FAME

(AF Archive / Alamy Stock Photo)

According to Google's Ranking Team, Andy Warhol is one of the 500 most famous people of all time and is the only truly famous artist of the last 60 years.[143] Even during his lifetime, his works were already making headlines for breaking auction records.

Having originally worked as a commercial graphic designer, Warhol's artistic breakthrough came with the 32 Campbell's Soup Cans exhibition at Ferus Gallery in Los Angeles in the summer of 1962. From the very beginning, his art was associated with creative PR. When his pictures of oversized soup cans were exhibited to the public for the first time, lined up along the gallery walls like supermarket displays, Warhol was initially ridiculed. His paintings were art, Warhol claimed, even if they didn't look like it. A rival gallery filled its display windows from top to bottom with

Campbell's soup cans, accompanied by the slogan: "The real thing for only 33 cents a can!" Warhol then took a photographer to the nearest supermarket and had a picture taken of him signing "the real thing," namely actual Campbell's soup cans. One of the photos was picked up by the leading news agency Associated Press and distributed halfway around the world.[144]

Warhol's promotional genius ensured that his soup can pictures were already a topic of conversation well before they were even exhibited. An article about the new Pop Art painters (Roy Lichtenstein, James Rosenquist and Warhol) was published in *Time* magazine on May 11, 1962. The article was accompanied by a photo of Warhol standing in front of a huge picture of a soup can, spooning soup from an original Campbell's can. His biographer Annette Spohn described this as "a marketing stunt of the first order, which shows once again that Warhol had a deep understanding of the laws of advertising and knew how to use them for his own purposes."[145] Just eight years later, in 1970, one of his Campbell's soup can paintings fetched the highest price ever paid for a work by a living American artist.[146]

The renowned art critic John Perreault wrote: "For millions, Warhol is the artist personified. The ghostly complexion, the silver-white hair, the dark glasses, and the leather jacket combine to make a memorable image, especially in conjunction with sensational headlines ... Some would maintain that Warhol's greatest art work is 'Andy Warhol.'"[147] Like almost no other artist, Warhol knew how to transform himself into a brand. That was the art he mastered best.

He believed in the omnipotence of the media and understood how to use it with aplomb. In an interview Warhol explained, "No one escapes the media. Media influences everyone. It's a very powerful weapon. George Orwell prophesied the potency of the media when he spoke of 'Big Brother is watching you' in his visionary novel *1984*."[148]

Warhol focused on his key competence. For him that meant marketing himself. He often had his works of art made by assistants and then just put his name on them. His biographer Annette Spohn wrote, "he was almost as great a genius at delegating work as he was in the art of marketing."[149] It was often difficult to tell who had actually made a "Warhol" work of art – Andy Warhol himself or one of his numerous assistants. Warhol proceeded no differently than the German Renaissance artist Lucas Cranach the Elder or the Italian master Leonardo da Vinci. The Andy Warhol Foundation for the Visual Arts was forced to set up its own authentication board, which concluded that if Warhol came up with the idea for a work and then ordered someone else to make the silkscreen, if he supervised the production process and confirmed it was what he wanted, then Warhol "created" the work in question.[150] But this was by no means always the case when the name "Warhol" appeared on a work of art. In interviews, he himself claimed that others had painted his pictures for him.[151]

A work of art, he affirmed on various occasions, didn't even need to be created by the artist himself. It was enough for the artist to add his signature after it came off the assembly line.[152] It was this philosophy that led Warhol to call his studio the Factory. He regularly left the execution of individual production steps, various parts of works or even entire works to assistants. "Warhol relegitimized and expanded the Renaissance practice of leaving parts of a work, or the whole thing, in the hands of others; to 'make' a work could mean simply to conceive it and approve its execution by assistants."[153]

However, Warhol did not really base his Factory approach on the *atelier* system of the Renaissance, but a modern variant, the studio system of Hollywood. His biographer Gary Indiana compares him to film producer Irving Thalberg, who was decisively involved in the creation of the work and the end result, but kept out of the actual fabrication process.[154] Warhol's biographer Wayne Koestenbaum aptly described Warhol's approach to art as a mixture of Picasso and Henry Ford: "Warhol's productivity escalated after he discovered that he could make more money by having assistants do his work while he drummed up new business; beneath this convenience lay the insight that transformed him into a mixture of Picasso and Henry Ford – the realization that the artist's atelier could be turned into a factory by mechanizing reproduction and minimizing manual touch."[155] Even when it came to the subject matter of his paintings, he often approached others for inspiration: "I was never embarrassed about asking someone, literally, 'What should I paint?'"[156] And what applied to his paintings also applied to his films. One of his "superstars" described the mood on set as follows: "It didn't matter who shot it or who 'directed' it, if Andy was in the room, it was Andy's film." The same actor also revealed to me that Andy's only direction to him, ever, "was to whisper in his ear: 'Too much plot!'"[157] Some Warhol films simply consisted of a person sleeping for many hours, filmed from a fixed, unchanged camera angle.

Warhol repeatedly gave the impression that he wanted to make himself superfluous. At public appearances, he often let himself be represented by a double, the actor Allen Midgette. When Warhol was invited to a series of college lectures, he sent the actor in his place; on another occasion he announced that he would be replaced by a robot. "The idea of replacing himself with a double, or cloning himself, was utterly consistent with Warhol's frequent assertion that anyone could do his paintings, that one could know everything about him by looking at the surfaces of his work, that there was nobody behind any of it; his famous statement that he wanted to be a machine underscored the techniques of mechanical reproduction with which he generated his art."[158] Of course, the press caught on to the stunt with the double, as the PR genius Warhol suspected they would, thereby creating yet another new story for the media to pounce on.

Warhol was brilliant at ensuring he was the center of attention. One of his methods was provocation. Once he was commissioned to make a mural for the U.S. pavilion at the 1964 World Expo in New York. The painting was supposed to highlight the United States as the exhibition's host – and Warhol decided to depict the 13 most wanted criminals in the country. In the run up to the Expo, government officials declared that they did not want such images to be used to represent the United States and, two weeks before the opening, Philip Johnson, the pavilion's architect, gave Warhol 24 hours to remove the offending images. One reason, allegedly, was that Nelson Rockefeller, the governor of New York, feared that the photos of the criminals (who were mostly of Italian descent) would offend many of those who had voted for him and cost him their support. Warhol then made a counterproposal – to replace the portraits of the criminals with 25 portraits of Robert Moses, the president of the World's Fair Corporation. But this proposal was also rejected. Warhol decided to paint over *Thirteen Most Wanted Men* with aluminum paint, which naturally attracted even more attention.

Even in the earliest years of his career as an artist, Warhol discovered that controversy was an effective way to generate publicity. In 1949 for the exhibition of the Pittsburgh Associated Artists, he submitted a picture of a boy with a finger jammed up one nostril. The title of the painting was *The Broad Gave Me My Face, But I Can Pick My Own Nose.* The jury, which had to decide on the picture, could not agree whether they should find the work "important" or simply dreadful. The jury's eventual rejection was later described as "Andy's first *succès de scandale.*"[159]

Warhol was a PR genius and was always thinking about how to turn every event in his life into a media story. On June 3, 1968, Warhol was almost assassinated. A militant women's rights activist pulled out two pistols and shot him several times. In her own words, she said she shot him because "he had too much power over my life."[160] Warhol was critically injured and was, at one point, even declared clinically dead, but survived after an operation lasting several hours. As soon as he was discharged from hospital, he considered how he could market the assassination attempt and its consequences in a way that would be appropriate for the media. His body was marked by numerous scars and Warhol decided to have it photographed by the famous portrait photographer Richard Avedon and painted by the portraitist Alice Neel. His commentary on the injuries is legendary: "I am so scarred I look like a Dior dress."[161]

Warhol was an eccentric and cultivated this image to the best of his ability. "Whenever somebody came up to the Factory," he says, "no matter how straight-looking he was, I'd ask him to take his pants off so I could photograph his cock and balls. It was surprising who'd let me and who wouldn't."[162] He let other men watch and sometimes a threesome developed.

Like other geniuses of self-marketing, he made every effort to use his clothes and appearance to create a distinctive brand. From the outset of his career, he understood the value of self-dramatization. He always wore dark turtlenecks, which emphasized his pale facial skin and prominent red nose.[163] In 1957, he underwent plastic surgery, which was still very unusual at the time. He started wearing toupees and sunglasses. Even though he was already earning a substantial amount and was certainly able to buy expensive clothes and luxury items, he reworked new suits and shoes until they looked worn out and fitted the image of the eccentric artist.[164]

Warhol wore a black leather jacket, tight black jeans (including pantyhose), T-shirts and high-heeled boots. His wigs were silver-gray, his Factory studio was silver, and this was the color of the Warhol brand.

On some occasions, he even used make-up to emphasize his Slavic features and paleness.[165] He later adopted a new signature style. He now wore velvet jackets, fancy shirts, ties and high heels. "Everyone's back to beautiful clothes. The hippie look is really gone," became his new motto.[166]

Unlike some of the other self-marketers portrayed in this book – such as Muhammad Ali or Arnold Schwarzenegger – Warhol was not the loud, extremely extroverted type. He is often even described as particularly shy. Roommates and friends from his early years characterized him as "whimsical, fey, sweet and charming, but painfully shy. About the only thing he ever said among a group of people was a whispered 'Hi!' as he spent long hours sitting in the apartment, drawing like a robot while the talk flowed around him ... 'He was an inarticulate, totally nonverbal young man.'"[167] His assistant Vito Giallo reported: "Even though he was shy and withdrawn at times, they all wanted to talk to him. And he would just listen. He was always like that, he wouldn't make any comments, never had much to offer, but everyone liked him."[168] But the description of Warhol as simply being "shy" does not do him justice. Koestenbaum put it more accurately when he described the contrast and duality of shyness and exhibitionism as characteristic of Warhol: "To certain observers, Warhol seemed quiet, passive, catatonic – as if he were holding back his true personality; on the other hand, he made sport of excessive revelation (through the mediation of accomplices). I found, in interviewing Warhol's associates, a consistent contrast between diffidence and exhibitionism, and I began to imagine that this duality reflected Andy's own character."[169]

This contradiction was characteristic of Warhol. In public or in face-to-face conversations the artist was often taciturn. "If Warhol wasn't crazy about talking (though he was, you only had to hear him on the phone to realize he was a champion blabbermouth), he had an authentic mania for writing and publishing everything he wouldn't say in a face-to-face conversation, or even on the phone."[170] This contradiction, the peculiar combination of shyness and exhibitionism, contributed to the enigmatic image that Warhol consciously cultivated. Other artists made elaborate efforts to explain their works of art and tell people what they were thinking. Warhol rejected this. Among his many artistic revolutions was that he transformed everyday consumer goods – such as soup cans or Coke bottles – into iconic objects of art. It was never clear whether he wanted to express love or loathing for these products, whether he was a left-wing critic of rampant American consumerism or whether he was fascinated by it – or perhaps both at the same time. The persona Warhol created "presented itself to the public as a glacial enigma," said Gary Indiana.[171]

Warhol repeatedly emphasized that his art speaks for itself, that there are no hidden meanings. "Other Pop Art artists," observed Indiana, "were more than happy to explain themselves and what they were trying to do. By withholding such explanations – or, more accurately, emitting clipped, comical, epigrammatic, and contradictory substitutes for more highfalutin pronouncements – Warhol became the most rarefied and famed exemplar of Pop Art and it's only real national, finally international, celebrity."[172] As Indiana explained, any interpretations of Warhol's art were mere attributions of the receptive viewer. Warhol even insisted that his works were not created to express or mean anything.[173]

Warhol did not want to become famous only among the educated elite who would philosophize about what an artist was hoping to say with a work of art, what secret messages could be read into it or what it revealed about the artist's psyche. Warhol understood that it was easier for him to become famous and make money if he created works of art that spoke for themselves. They should be beautiful in their own right without requiring them to "mean" anything. "All they revealed, really, was that a soup can grabbed off a supermarket shelf could be beautiful exactly as it was, in all its monumentalized banality."[174]

For interviewers, he was a very difficult interviewee, which actually made him a far more interesting interlocutor. He made a habit of refusing to answer questions, sometimes by simply repeating the question back to his interviewer as his "answer." Not infrequently he switched roles and began to interview his interviewer. His answers often made no sense, but it was precisely this unusual, enigmatic and surprising aspect that made him such a sought-after interviewee for media outlets up and down the country. In the collection of interviews "I'll be your mirror," the editor Kenneth Goldsmith has collected numerous examples of the unexpected twists and turns interviews with Warhol frequently took. Warhol often answered questions with a simple "I don't know." Here are just a few examples:

"What is Pop Art trying to say" – "I don't know."

"How did you get started making movies?" "Uh… I don't know…"

"What is your role, your function in directing a Warhol film?" "I don't know. I'm trying to figure it out."[175]

Warhol turned his habit of giving unexpected, crazy and provocative answers in interviews into one of his most distinct trademarks. For a 1970s art anthology, renowned artists were asked for their thoughts on other well-known artists. When Warhol was asked about the significance of the abstract expressionist Barnett Newman, he answered, "The only way I knew Barney was I think Barney went to more parties than I did."[176] And when asked for his opinion of Pablo Picasso, he said, "Ah, the only thing I can really relate to is his daughter Paloma … I'm just glad he had a wonderful daughter like Paloma."[177] And in relation to Jasper Johns, the pioneer of Pop Art, he could only think of "Ohhh, uh, he makes such great lunches. He does this great thing with chicken. He puts parsley *inside* the chicken."[178] Sometimes he also used interviews to flirt with the interviewer or even make direct sexual advances.[179]

His refusal to accept rules was a manifestation of Warhol's childlike side. Like many other geniuses of self-marketing, he had never really put his childhood behind him, as his biographers note, "Warhol's capacious intellect was tweaked by the emotional affect of an eight-year-old. His insight and cunning deserve acknowledgement; so does his awesome immaturity. His knowingness about people matched his inability to sustain mature relationships."[180] Even as an adult, he had avoided breaking away from his infantile attachments – and had thus established himself in a state of persistent childhood.[181] It is also striking that he lived with his mother in an apartment until her death.

Warhol was desperate to become famous. The subject of fame and celebrity occupied him like no other. He became "synonymous with the culture of celebrity-for-its-own-sake," as one of his biographers wrote.[182] Even as a child, he had an insatiable appetite for movie magazines. He collected "personalized" autographed photographs of film stars.[183] This created a self-perpetuating spiral: he systematically sought out the company of famous people and his rising fame made it increasingly easy for him to meet celebrities, which in turn increased his own fame. Parties played a crucial role in his life. "On the one hand, the invitations showed how popular and hip you were in the scene, and on the other hand they were an opportunity for him to meet celebrities – his great childhood dream and always the focus of his life."[184]

Working for famous people increased his own fame. One example is his work for the record company of his friend Mick Jagger of the Rolling Stones. It was Warhol who designed the unusual cover for the album Sticky Fingers with the picture of a pair of jeans on the front and back and a zipper that could be pulled down to reveal a tantalizing glimpse of white underwear beneath. "With virtuosity, Warhol took advantage of the celebrity status of his friends and clients for his own publicity and again proved his impressive talent for self-marketing."[185]

He increasingly moved in celebrity circles, in a glamorous whirl of movie stars, politicians, fashion czars, famous musicians and celebrities of all stripes. He socialized with Liz Taylor, Jackie Onassis, Shirley MacLaine, Paloma Picasso, Henry Kissinger, Jimmy Carter, Yves Saint Laurent, Diana Ross, Pierre Cardin and John Lennon.[186] On the one hand, Warhol was one of them, but on the other, he always kept a distance. He usually had a camera and a cassette recorder with him to record images and sound.

When choosing the motifs for his art, he always carefully considered how much of a media splash they would create. In his first large exhibition in New York, he exhibited pictures of Marilyn Monroe, Elvis Presley and accidents (e.g. car crashes). He chose Monroe and Presley because they were idols for millions of Americans and everyone knew them. He demonstrated exquisite timing in creating and exhibiting his portraits. Only a few days after Marilyn Monroe's death on August 4, 1962, he acquired the actress's publicity photo from the 1950s. Without further ado, he cropped the image to cut away the lower part of her bust and had a silkscreen made from this template, which he did not modify in any other way.

Later in his career, he accepted a large number of commissions from famous people who wanted their very own Warhol portrait. The price of $25,000 doesn't seem too high from a modern perspective, but adjusted for inflation this would still be $165,000 per picture in today's money. From the beginning of the 1970s, he made about 50 to 100 portraits of this kind per year. Many of the people were famous, but if someone could afford one, he would also make portraits of unknown clients.[187]

His mercenary approach increasingly attracted opprobrium in

the art world. Critics saw nothing but artistic stagnation in Warhol's endless variations and in his constant series. "Too many of his commissioned portraits had a slapped-together and rebarbative ugliness, uncharacteristically lifeless blocks of color and thick smears of arbitrary brushwork."[188] And indeed, he lost much of his creative energy after the assassination attempt. His status as an artist has always been questioned, but "Warhol's celebrity never went into eclipse."[189]

Tools Andy Warhol used to build his brand:

1. Radical violation of generally accepted rules: He painted oversized soup cans and blithely claimed they were art.

2. Creative PR ideas: When a competing gallery exhibited real soup cans to ridicule Warhol's art, he commissioned photographers and signed the original soup cans at the nearest supermarket. The photos went around the world.

3. The artist as a machine, the artist's studio as a factory: Warhol had many of his works of art made by assistants before adding his signature as they rolled off the production line. He focused on his core competence: building himself as a brand.

4. When invited to lectures and parties, he sometimes sent a double in his place – ensuring that he was part of the conversation even when he wasn't there.

5. Provocation: When he was commissioned to provide art for the U.S. pavilion at the World Expo, he lined the walls with pictures of the country's 13 most wanted criminals. In response to the ensuing scandal, he had them all sprayed with silver paint and thus became a topic of conversation again.

6. He exploited every aspect of his life for self-marketing, even his scars: After an assassination attempt, his whole body was riddled

with bullet wounds. Warhol decided to have his disfigured body photographed by a famous portrait photographer and painted by the portraitist Alice Neel.

7. Warhol was obsessed with celebrities, sought their company and thereby increased his own fame.

8. Breaking the rules in interviews: Warhol typically gave totally surprising answers in interviews. Sometimes he began to interview the interviewer or made sexual advances. Or simply gave nonsensical answers.

9. He also turned his appearance into a feature of his brand, for example, by wearing a silver wig that matched the color he had chosen for his brand.

10. Warhol cultivated an inscrutable, enigmatic and contradictory image: The man who went to church every Sunday yet made pornographic films, the artist who claimed his works of art were made by others.

11. His persona – an odd combination of extreme shyness and unrestrained exhibitionism – made him an unmistakable brand.

CHAPTER THREE

KARL LAGERFELD:
ME, MYSELF AND I

(Allstar Picture Library Ltd / Alamy Stock Photo)

Many people define themselves through their profession, Karl Lagerfeld even called himself a "professional person" – as opposed to a "person of leisure."[190] And he had so many professions that it would be unfair to identify him exclusively with just one of them. He once said in an interview that the job title to describe everything he did had yet to be invented. "His profession changes like a chameleon," is how Paul Sahner described Lagerfeld's mastery of many domains in his biography. "Fashion designer, discoverer of top models, photographer, interior designer, parfumier, entrepreneur, silent film maker, lord of the manor, gallery owner, author, porcelain collector, advertising guru, PR man, publisher and bookseller."[191] Lagerfeld was Lagerfeld. Like almost no-one before or since, he established himself as a brand and narcissism as his religion. "Me, myself and I" was his motto, according to Sahner.[192] During the course of his life, Lagerfeld explained, he had turned himself into a caricature, into a living work of art: "I am no longer human. I am an abstraction. I am both the puppet and the puppeteer. And that's how I like it. I have little to do with earthly problems."[193] Lagerfeld once greeted a journalist sympathetically with the remark, "I was once a mere mortal like you."[194] But that's exactly what he never wanted to be – a mere mortal like everyone else. "I no longer feel like a human being."[195]

Such sentences would seem extremely odd if they came from anyone else. But coming from Lagerfeld, we accept them, maybe because of his great sense of self-irony. He was proud to be on a diet in which he lost 40 percent of his weight, but he also said afterwards: "When I stand in front of the mirror without clothes, it tells me that I have something of the appearance of a medical student's anatomical skeleton."[196] Lagerfeld claimed that he was always the first to laugh at himself and was convinced of the therapeutic benefits of not taking yourself too seriously: "Everyone can be grotesque in certain situations. If you pay attention, you will notice it, too. As long as you are honest with yourself."[197]

He had no fear of anyone confronting him with one of his earlier statements or pointing out his logical inconsistencies. He immunized himself against criticism by repeatedly emphasizing that what he said was only valid if he had just said it. "Please don't take what I say so seriously. If I say something today, I may not remember it tomorrow. Tomorrow I'll be a completely different person."[198]

Whether Lagerfeld really wanted people to take him less seriously and not pay such close attention to his opinions is doubtful. For Lagerfeld, what came across as self-irony was more of a strategy in self-marketing. It allowed him to display a level of arrogance and snobbery that would not be accepted from anyone else. Had he ever written an autobiography, he wanted to write it in English and was adamant he would never have allowed it to be translated: "If people in France or Germany want to read my autobiography but don't know English, I say, 'Then this book isn't for them!'"[199] On another occasion, he explained that since most of his trips were paid for by corporations, he always traveled by private jet. "If I'm not worthy of a private jet to someone, I don't have to go there. I take that liberty. It also confirms that the companies value me and my work."

Otherwise, he'd rather stay home and read a book or do nothing.[200]

So, who was Karl Lagerfeld? He was born in Hamburg in 1933, but cultivated an air of mystery around his true date of birth. He reported that, even as a child he was told, "You are unique." With a characteristic lack of humility, he admitted, "And I probably believed it, too."[201] As a student, he wanted to be different from his classmates, even if that meant them teasing him for it. "Have you ever looked in the mirror? It's your own fault," said his mother when he complained about being ridiculed by his classmates. Lagerfeld conceded, "She was right. The other boys had crew cuts, I was going for exotic blooms, with long hair and big curls."[202] He wanted to be different from his classmates, who turned up at school in the post-war period in worn and tatty clothes. Lagerfeld, in contrast, appeared at school with tailor-made jackets, impeccable shirts with starched collars and silk ties.[203] Coming from a wealthy manufacturer's family, he could afford such clothes. Later he went into bodybuilding, posing on the beach with his well-toned body.[204]

Because he loved sweets so much, he gained a lot of weight in a later phase of his life and topped the scales at over 100 kilos. He celebrated his weight loss cure – he lost 42 kilos in 13 months [205] – as a public event and let the whole world join in. He did nothing in secret, he shared everything with the world at large, even his diet. He decided to co-write a book about his diet with his doctor. His studio manager Arnaud Maillard was surprised: "I don't know what his real intention is: to write a bestseller or make himself the subject of media attention? I just can't imagine a fashion designer of his stature getting excited about the idea of publishing a book about the minutiae of his diet."[206] But Lagerfeld's book became a bestseller and journalists flocked to interview him – about his dietary formula. "He complains for the sake of appearance, but still throws himself into the media flood," said Maillard, who worked for Lagerfeld for 15 years.[207]

Like other self-marketing geniuses, Lagerfeld pretended to be annoyed by the media, and often claimed that he was completely indifferent to what people said about him. Of course, that was not true. He bought and read all the newspapers that contained articles about him. And he courted journalists as few celebrities do. Paul Sahner, then editor-in-chief of the German celebrity gossip magazine *Bunte*, reported how Lagerfeld invited him to Biarritz and how impressed he was when the chauffeur who picked him up from the airport handed him a handwritten letter on egg-yolk yellow paper: "The fact that Karl, a busy man, finds the time to prepare so warmly for my stay with him, proves his extraordinary qualities as a host. He thinks of everything, just like a master of ceremonies at the court of the Sun King – fulfilling both roles himself."[208]

In the course of his life, Lagerfeld built his public image – the Lagerfeld brand – around a series of distinctive features. He did not establish his brand overnight or with a single conscious decision – he cultivated his celebrity over the years. "I don't put on a costume like Charlie Chaplin. My hairstyle, my sunglasses, they have all come to me over the years. Slowly but surely, I have become like a caricature of myself."[209]

As he developed his signature style, a distinctive trademark emerged: The fingerless gloves, the powdered braid, the stand-up collar, the sunglasses, and, at times, a fan. Thanks to his iconic image, Lagerfeld certainly made life easy for caricaturists. But the Lagerfeld brand was about far more than just his outward appearance. He also became famous for his irreverent sayings and distinctive way of speaking. Lagerfeld, said Sahner, was the grand master of staccato melodies. "He pronounces words rapidly, and frequently changes tempo from hasty to languid. Sometimes his sentences dance bossa nova, sometimes they sound almost pastoral."[210]

At the beginning of the 1950s, Lagerfeld moved to Paris and worked for numerous fashion houses, including Balmain, Patou and Chloé. In the 80s, he made his big breakthrough as creative director and chief designer of Chanel. The company, which had been founded by Coco Chanel, had a somewhat stale image at the time. Lagerfeld gave the label a legendary revamp and transformed it into a billion-dollar, global fashion powerhouse. "I made Chanel what it is today," said Lagerfeld. "Without me, this fashion house would have long closed. The last heir, the one who came for me, said, 'Either you get in or I close.'"[211]

But it would be doing Lagerfeld a disservice to reduce him to the role of fashion designer for some of the world's most luxurious brands. A list of everything Lagerfeld turned his hand to would more than fill this chapter. He designed a Steiff teddy bear and pens for Faber-Castell as well as limited edition Diet Coke bottles, bracelets, necklaces and brooches for the Swarovski company, the famous perfume, Chloé for Women, and his own range of perfumes under his own name. He worked as a costume designer for theater and opera and as a photographer; he designed advertising campaigns for the Dom Pérignon champagne brand and for the Volkswagen Phaeton model; he founded his own publishing house and made a name for himself with his book collection, which included 300,000 works. He struck the right balance between creating exclusive fashion and designing a collection and a perfume for the Swedish mass-market fashion chain H&M. He combined an air of elitism with egalitarian values: "The upper ten thousand have always been the victims of their own snobbery. Only the most expensive is good enough for them. But it is important not to look down on the 'masses.' We need to offer affordable options. You can still look chic while buying cheap."[212]

Lagerfeld valued freedom above all else. Early in his career, he achieved something that had eluded many designers before him, namely to work for several fashion houses at the same time. "He quickly became a man who could work with anyone. This is an enviable quality that only a few are granted," Sahner wrote. Sahner described Lagerfeld's eclectic approach as follows, "A camel's-hair coat for Max Mara, yes, I'd be delighted, camel hair is my favorite material. A fur coat for Fendi, wonderful, I love stuffed animals. A collection for Patou, well, that also exists as golf fashion. A costume for the lady who favors Chloé. Fabulous. It's almost ready."[213]

He created so much because his business model gave him the freedom to focus on what he was best at – designing. He left everything else to others. And in this way, he earned much more than he would have earned with his own brand or even as a designer working exclusively for one company. "With a myriad of contracts and licenses and cross-connections, he manages to get the others to take the load off his shoulders while he keeps his creative fire burning. He designs bags, shoes, fabrics, wallpaper, glasses, knitwear, furs, expensive clothes, cheap clothes – sometimes under his own name, but often not."[214]

According to Lagerfeld, it was completely natural for him to be creative. "The more you do, the more ideas you have. Like a pianist, the more you play, the more natural it becomes to improvise. If I sketch all the time, I find new ideas."[215] On the one hand, ideas just came to him, on the other, he didn't sit back and wait for inspiration to strike. He once explained how he was looking for a new idea for a bathing suit. He sat down and told himself not to get up until he had designed 50 new swimsuits. After three hours, his 50 designs were ready, but he kept going anyway.[216]

Discipline and a ceaseless work ethic were among his most important traits, despite the fact that he lived in a hedonistic world, full of seductions and temptations. Lagerfeld did not succumb to these temptations. He didn't smoke, didn't take drugs, and almost never drank. He probably knew that he needed this self-discipline because he sensed that he was prone to addiction. At certain periods in his life he regularly drank several liters of Diet Coke a day and ate vast quantities of sweets.

Fashion designer Wolfgang Joop said of Lagerfeld: "You could really take his advice to heart: You have to keep your own feelings and addictions in check, because otherwise you will become a victim of the scene. After all, many around him have become victims ... How to deal with discipline, how to keep one's composure, he demonstrated that *par excellence*. In that respect, he's the greatest phenomenon I've ever met. Ingenious."[217]

Many of his friends died of AIDS, others suffered from the consequences of excessive drug use. He observed this and abstained with iron discipline. When he praised other people, he liked to praise their self-control. For example, when describing one of the models he discovered, Claudia Schiffer, he said that unlike many other models, she had had an "iron discipline": "The others had more fun, but less discipline."[218]

This discipline increasingly became a central feature of the Lagerfeld brand. You can't imagine him being casual about anything, and his statement on a German television talk show that "if you wear sweatpants, you have lost control of your life" was probably quoted more often than any other of the many Lagerfeld *bon mots*. "People tell me: 'You are German. You have lots of self-discipline.' ... I am much worse. I am an auto-fascist, a dictator, who puts myself under pressure. When it comes to me, I don't tolerate democracy. There is no discussion, I give orders. I don't suffer much from that either. Orders are orders, period."[219]

And yet it would be a great mistake to understand Lagerfeld's indomitable willpower as meaning that he had to force himself to work. He needed discipline to resist temptation, to follow his diet – and he made sure that strict discipline prevailed in his studio, where he controlled everything with paramilitary rigor. A studio manager made sure that all of Lagerfeld's instructions were strictly adhered to. The pressure to meet deadlines was brutal.[220]

Nevertheless, Lagerfeld frequently observed that designing came naturally. "I don't know what it is to be stressed. I know only what it is to be dressed. I'm in the fashion business."[221] If discipline means forcing yourself to do things that you can't stand, then Lagerfeld did not need this kind of discipline at work. "We do what we enjoy doing all day anyway," he said. "Designing is as natural to me as breathing."[222] He thought about his work while he was asleep, dreamt about it and wrote down his thoughts when he got up. On one occasion, he reported: "I dreamed a whole collection and the next morning, I drew it completely. Everything worked out fine."[223]

What drove Lagerfeld? Was it money, as some said? After all, he became one of the richest men in Paris and he always openly admitted that he loved making money. Or was it the pursuit of fame, of recognition? "I am more celebrated than Galliano and all the others. No one is as successful as me. No one can keep up. I can't cross the street anymore. And how the autograph hunters crowd me. Mail comes in from all over the world with requests for autographs. It's unbelievable." Having said this, he was quick to add what most famous people say in a similar vein: He was amused by the attention and claimed not to understand the public's obsession with him.[224]

When Lagerfeld claims not to understand the excitement around him and his brand, he is about as believable as the other geniuses of self-marketing in this book who made similar claims. Maillard remembers walking into a Diesel store with Lagerfeld and all eyes were on him. "Finally, a group of smiling Japanese dare to approach, hand on mouth and pens at the ready. Other, somewhat intimidated customers quickly follow. Karl winks at me briefly: 'Look, even the young people know me! Not bad, is it?'"[225]

Yes, every celebrity is sometimes overwhelmed by the hype about themselves and the loss of privacy that comes with it. But Lagerfeld, and other stars of his stature, accept these consequences, because the alternative would be unbearable: to fall through the cracks of history as an unknown, to be indistinguishable from the masses. Lagerfeld even justified his decision not to have children by saying that he always considered himself an absolutely unique specimen and therefore did not feel the slightest need to "clone this uniqueness."[226]

In order to attract media attention, he deliberately overstepped the mark and made provocative, controversial statements. In 1993, he had Claudia Schiffer walk down the runway, wearing verses from the Koran across her chest. There were harsh protests, because Muslims interpreted this stunt as disparaging the Koran and the life of the Prophet. To calm the waves of indignation, an apology was issued. Upon reflection, Lagerfeld observed, "Scandal only hurts those who have none."[227]

While on the one hand he sought to cause a stir with his provocative statements, on the other, he captured the zeitgeist with his fashion – and shaped it in his own image. If you make it your *raison d'être* to always swim against the current, you will not be successful, whether in business or in the fashion world. The same can be said of people who always swim with the current. The art lies in always staying ahead of the curve and constantly reinventing yourself – while at same time maintaining an unmistakable brand core. "This challenges you to retain your own personality, but at the same time to develop with the zeitgeist. To create something new without repeating oneself is even more interesting."[228]

In its Lagerfeld obituary, the German news magazine *Der Spiegel* addressed the Lagerfeld phenomenon: "He invented himself, transformed himself into an art figure until he was a global brand." He was the "pioneer of an age in which staging and image are everything. Radical, free and unique."[229]

He didn't mind being described as a narcissist. In fact, he hardly tried to hide his narcissism. Maillard reports that Lagerfeld often did not even look at his colleagues when he spoke to them. When he answered, he looked at himself in the mirror over the shoulders of the people he was talking to. Even during fittings, he was primarily interested only in himself. "His eagle eye needs only a fraction of a second to decide on a model. Unfortunately. Because despite his outstanding professionalism, the couturier gives the impression that he is not interested in anything or anyone apart from his own appearance." He took every photo shoot as an opportunity to take portraits of himself, and after every session a new self-portrait landed on the desk of Karl's communications manager, which he was to pass on to journalists.[230]

When Lagerfeld was asked whether he was thinking of perhaps

setting up a charitable foundation, he replied that he had nothing to gain because: "All that I am begins and ends with me."[231] Presumably, any other public figure would have been scolded as a ruthless egoist if they had dared to express what Lagerfeld took for granted: "I want to have a comfortable life. Without problems. I am my beginning and my end. And what I want to achieve, I determine myself. I don't have to be considerate of anyone, I don't have to take responsibility for anyone."[232] Perhaps people forgave him such statements because they secretly thought and sometimes felt similarly, but would never have dared to say so openly? Perhaps some people also thought that, in truth, he could not have meant it that way, and that this was just one of his deliberately provocative *bon mots*, which should not be taken so seriously, let alone literally. Lagerfeld's approach to life can be summarized in two principles: boundless freedom and the irrepressible urge to constantly evolve. "Happiness," he said, "is a question of order and discipline. I am the result of what I myself have painted and imagined, what I wanted and I decided to be."[233]

How did he manage to ensure that people did not get tired of him despite his omnipresence, as is the case with many other celebrities? One explanation is that he constantly reinvented himself and thus did not become boring. He was driven by the power of productive discontent, or, to put it in his own words: "I'm never satisfied. I always think that I could do better ... a better show, a better collection, everything could always be better."[234]

Another explanation is that despite all the interviews he willingly gave, he managed to keep something secret. Sunglasses also meant that nobody could really see inside him. The man who hung mirrors everywhere so that he could always look at himself made every effort to hide his eyes, the "mirror of the soul." Lagerfeld cannot be pigeonholed by what he did – no single job title does him justice – nor by the views he expressed, which he often relativized within moments of pronouncing them. With other people, the older they get, the more they start talking about the past. Lagerfeld found that depressing and once said that you could kill yourself if you thought your best times were behind you. "I only think about the future. That's probably because of my job. I don't know what clothes I made yesterday, and I don't care."[235]

Tools Karl Lagerfeld used to build his brand:

1. As a designer, he also designed his own image, which included his outward appearance: the fingerless gloves, the powdered braid, the stand-up collar, the sunglasses and, at times, a fan. He once observed that he had transformed himself into a caricature.

2. His *bon mots* and his unusual sayings ("If you wear sweatpants, you have lost control of your life") had a high recognition value.

3. He was not ashamed of his narcissism, but celebrated it to the full. By combining this with (perhaps only affected) self-irony, he made boundless selfishness and self-love acceptable.

4. The staccato rhythm of his speech became an unmistakable trademark.

5. Lagerfeld celebrated radical freedom and individualism. He combined the freedom of not having to obey anyone with extreme self-discipline.

6. He always remained somewhat mysterious – an effect enhanced by the sunglasses he used to hide his eyes.

7. He combined an extremely elitist demeanor and the air of a nobleman from centuries gone by with a willingness to embrace popular culture (he designed affordable products for H&M).

CHAPTER FOUR

STEPHEN HAWKING:
MASTER OF THE UNIVERSE

(JEP Celebrity Photos / Alamy Stock Photo)

In 1959, Stephen Hawking began studying mathematics and physics at Oxford, his birthplace, and in 1962 he was awarded his bachelor's degree. In his final year at Oxford, he realized something was wrong. Twice, he lost his balance and took tumbles for no apparent reason. Worried, he went to the doctor, whose only advice was, "Lay off the beer." After graduating from Oxford, Hawking moved to Cambridge to write his PhD thesis in cosmology. But Hawking's health continued to deteriorate: "At Christmas, when I went skating on the lake at St. Albans, I fell over and couldn't get up. My mother noticed these problems and took me to the family doctor. He referred me to a specialist, and shortly after my twenty-first birthday I went into the hospital for testing."[236]

For weeks, Hawking, whose father was a tropical medicine researcher and whose mother was an economist, was subjected to a wide variety of tests. The doctors didn't tell him what he was suffering from, but he soon realized that he had an incurable disease that was likely to end his life within a few years.

Eventually, his doctors told him that he was suffering from amyotrophic lateral sclerosis (ALS), a disease that causes the nerve cells of the brain and spinal cord to first atrophy and then scar or harden. He learned that people with this disease gradually lose the ability to control their movements, speak, eat and, ultimately, breathe. His doctors then issued a dire prognosis and told him he probably only had two years to live – in fact he lived another 50.[237]

Of course, the news of his illness came as a massive shock. Hawking initially descended into a severe depression, which became even deeper as he spent hours listening to Wagner operas at full volume. "Holed up in his room at Cambridge, Hawking listened to music, read science fiction, struggled with terrifying nightmares and showed little interest in his PhD."[238] But looking back, the news about his illness also had a very positive effect on him. "My dreams at the time," Hawking recalled, "were rather disturbed. Before my condition was diagnosed, I had been very bored with life. There had not seemed to be anything worth doing. But shortly after I came out of the hospital, I dreamed that I was going to be executed. I suddenly realized that there were a lot of worthwhile things I could do if I was reprieved."[239]

To his great surprise, he found that he enjoyed his life more now than ever before. This was partly because he had just fallen in love. And he knew that, if he was to marry, he had to find a job and finish his PhD. "I therefore started working for the first time in my life. To my surprise, I found I liked it."[240]

While studying at Oxford, Hawking admits he was rather lazy. His courses were easy, he confesses, and he got used to things falling right into his lap. But now that his disease had been diagnosed, he buried himself in his research. It was his research, together with his wife Jane, whom he had married in 1965, that helped him discover meaning in life.

In this, Hawking displays one of the key characteristics he shares with many great figures, namely to turn a bad situation into a good one, and to draw energy from even the most debilitating crises. Rather than feeling sorry for himself and complaining about his disability, he soon came to see it as a great advantage: "I haven't had to lecture or teach undergraduates, and I haven't had to sit in on tedious and time-consuming committees. So I have been able to devote myself completely to research."[241] In his opinion, disabled people should "concentrate on things that their handicap doesn't prevent them from doing and not regret those they can't do."[242] According to his biographers Michael White and John Gribbin, Hawking would never have reached such dizzying heights so quickly if he had been expected to spend vast amounts of time on committees, conferences or overseeing undergraduate applications.[243]

Hawking quickly made a name for himself in the scientific community. In 1974, he predicted that black holes would emit thermal radiation, which subsequently became known as Hawking radiation. In the same year, he was also elected a fellow of the prestigious Royal Society – at that time he was not even a professor, just a research assistant. Three years later, he was promoted to the position of professor. "My work on black holes had given me hope that we would discover a theory of everything."[244] A series of important discoveries followed, for which Hawking received numerous scientific honors and accolades.

Undoubtedly a great scientist, Hawking was well aware of his status within the scientific community. "To my colleagues, I'm just another physicist, but to the wider public I became possibly the best-known scientist in the world."[245] It is not possible to explain Hawking's fame in terms of his scientific discoveries alone, especially as their true ramifications – as with Einstein – were impossible for most people to understand. Hawking enjoyed a far higher profile than many Nobel Prize winners, despite the fact that he never won the Nobel Prize, most likely because according to the award's guidelines, any eligible discovery needs to be confirmed experimentally, which was not possible with Hawking's theoretical physics. His theories and predictions were based on mathematics, but they could not be confirmed by experiment.

And when it came to his standing within the scientific community, Hawking was correct. To his peers, he was by no means the exceptional scientist the public perceived him to be. For instance, a survey of physicists around the millennium by *Physics World* magazine did not even place him among the top ten most important living physicists.[246]

In contrast, the public – and presumably Hawking himself – had a very different perception, one more in keeping with his cameo in an episode of *Star Trek: The Next Generation*, where he appeared in a virtual poker game with two of the most iconic scientists in history, Sir Isaac Newton and Albert Einstein.[247] So, how did Hawking, fully aware that his colleagues saw him as just one physicist among many, become the most famous scientist of his era? Well, Hawking provides the answer in his autobiography: "This is partly because scientists, apart from Einstein, are not widely known rock stars, and partly because I fit the stereotype of a disabled genius. I can't disguise myself with a wig and dark glasses – the wheelchair gives me away."[248]

But no scientist, no matter how groundbreaking their research, could possibly become a global cultural icon and celebrity without actively pursuing fame at least to some extent, even if like Hawking, they are in a wheelchair or have a rare disease. To achieve the kind of fame Hawking enjoyed requires actively cultivating a public image – as we saw with Einstein.

At the start of his career, Hawking was smart in choosing his field of research. He based his decision on the fact that, at that time, elementary particle physics was a highly regarded and rapidly changing field that attracted most of the best scientific minds in the world. By contrast, cosmology and general relativity were stuck where they had been in the 1930s.[249] Hawking realized that it was easier for him to attract attention with new research and began to establish himself as an authority on a subject that captured everyone's imagination – black holes. A black hole is a region of spacetime where gravity is so strong that nothing – no matter, no light and no information – can escape. A black hole can be formed by the death of a massive star when, at the end of its life, the core becomes unstable and gravitationally collapses inward upon itself to a point of zero volume and infinite density called the singularity.

According to Hawking's biographers Michael White and John Gribbin: "He was becoming the black hole cosmonaut trapped in a crippled body, piercing the mysteries of the Universe with the mind of a latter-day Einstein, going where even angels feared to tread. With the arrival of black holes in the public consciousness, the mystique that had begun to gather around him in Cambridge at the end of the sixties started to extend beyond the cloistered limits of the physics community. Newspaper articles and TV documentaries about black holes started to appear, and Stephen Hawking began to be seen as the man to talk to."[250]

As with Einstein, the media and the general public were inspired by the mysterious nature of his theories, which were essentially incomprehensible to non-experts. The fact that these cosmological messages were being delivered by a man with a mysterious illness – a man who communicated with ordinary mortals in an unearthly, computerized voice – served to heighten the overall effect.

As a result of his illness, Hawking's speech became progressively more indistinct and slurred. Even his children had difficulty understanding him. After a bout of pneumonia, he needed a life-saving tracheostomy. From then on, he completely lost the ability to speak. His only means of communication at first was to spell out words, one letter at a time, by raising his eyebrows when someone pointed to the correct letter on a spelling card.[251] He later used a computer program and a speech synthesizer. A special device allowed him to select blocks of words and letters, which were then converted into spoken words by a speech synthesizer. As time went by, he got better and better at using the system, and although it only generated a maximum of 15 words per minute, he was able to communicate better than he could before the tracheostomy.[252] As his biographer Joel Levy observes, Hawking's synthesized voice became one of his trademarks and he even copyrighted it.[253]

Even once he mastered his voice synthesizer, he still found other, sometimes more direct, methods of communication. Hawking, who was famous for not suffering fools lightly, simply drove his wheelchair over his interlocutor's toes whenever they said something that annoyed him. And if he felt that someone was wasting his time, he would abruptly turn round and steer his wheelchair out of the room.[254]

The fact that Hawking became famous did not happen by accident, and certainly not against his will. On the contrary. He tinkered with his own legend and was – like Einstein – a genius of self-marketing. For example, he made a big deal of the fact that he was born on January 8, 1942, exactly 300 years after the death of Galileo. Although he did always add that about 200,000 other children were probably born on the same day, his birthday was part of his self-crafted legend.[255]

Even when it came to his earliest books, which he wrote for a scientific readership and not – as was the case with his later publications – as popular scientific works, he refused to behave like a typical scientist. Ahead of the publication of his third book, *Superspace and Supergravity,*

Hawking had a series of heated arguments with his publisher about the book's cover. Hawking wanted the publisher to use a color photograph of a drawing from the blackboard in his office for the dust jacket of both the hardback and paperback editions of the book.[256] His publisher refused, claiming they had never had a color cover on a book like Hawking's. They insisted that the costs could not be justified given the scientific nature of the book and its expected sales figures, and claimed that the cover itself would have no impact on the number of copies they would sell. Hawking threatened to withdraw his book completely if the publisher did not agree to use his cover. In the end, Hawking prevailed.[257]

After having written a handful of scientific publications, Hawking decided to turn his hand to popular science books. Allegedly, financial motives, including the high cost of his day-to-day care, played a major role in his decision.[258] This is probably true, but an even greater motivation for Hawking was that he wanted to become world famous – not only in scientific circles, but far beyond: "If I was going to spend the time and effort to write a book, I wanted it to get to as many people as possible."[259]

Hawking decided to write a bestseller. He explained to his agent that he wanted to write a book that would sell in airport bookstores. The agent replied that there was no chance of that – it might sell respectable numbers to academics and students, but a book like Hawking's could never succeed in Jeffrey Archer territory.[260]

Unlike many other scientists, Hawking listened carefully to the advice of his editors. In one of their earliest discussions about Hawking's new book for the popular market, his editor explained: "It's still far too technical, Stephen. Look at it this way, Steve – every equation will halve your sales." Hawking, who spent the entire day working with mathematical formulae, did not understand the objection and wanted to know why his editor would say something like that. His editor responded, "Well, when people look at a book in a shop, they just flick through it to decide if they want to read it. You've got equations on practically every page. When they look at this, they'll say, 'This book's got sums in it,' and put it back on the shelf."[261] Hawking followed his editor's advice, but he ultimately decided not to publish the new book with his previous publishing house – the academic publisher Cambridge University Press – but with a larger publisher which could reach a wider audience and pay a bigger advance and more lucrative royalties on book sales. Hawking and his agent negotiated with several major publishers and finally reached an agreement with the American publisher Bantam. One of the things that clinched the deal was the publisher's assurance that the book would be available at every airport bookstore in America. "Hawking loved the idea. The fact that his book was with one of the world's biggest publishers gave him a real thrill."[262]

Most authors don't like editors who demand lots of changes to their books, and certainly not editors who call for almost a complete rewrite of the entire book. And for Hawking, who was not able to write at the same speed as other authors, these extensive rewrites were particularly laborious and time-consuming. But Hawking was determined to write a bestseller and made every effort to write the best book he possibly could. His new editor convinced him to rewrite the book so that even non-scientists could understand it. "Each time I sent him a rewritten chapter," recalled Hawking, "he sent back a long list of objections and questions he wanted me to clarify. At times I thought the process would never end. But he was right: it is a much better book as a result."[263]

His former editor at his previous academic publisher made sure to warn Hawking: "Do ensure that you are quite certain that, if the aim is to make money and sell lots of books, you don't mind the marketing techniques." When Hawking asked him what he meant, the editor answered: "Well, I wouldn't put it past them to market it as 'Aren't cripples marvelous?' You've got to go into it with your eyes open."[264]

The book was published in the United States as *A Brief History of Time* and didn't need any such primitive marketing techniques to become a bestseller and far exceed the publisher's expectations. It spent 147 weeks on *The New York Times* bestseller list, a record-breaking 237 weeks on the London *Times* bestseller list[265] and, in Germany, 41 weeks on the *Spiegel* bestseller list. The book has since been translated into 40 languages and has sold more than 10 million copies worldwide.

Why was the book so successful? Hawking wasn't entirely sure and thought that most of the reviews, although favorable, were not particularly illuminating. As a rule, they all followed the same formula. They started by highlighting the fact that Stephen Hawking suffers from a serious illness, is in a wheelchair and can hardly move his fingers. Then they pointed out that, despite all this, he has written a book about the biggest question of all time: Where do we come from and where are we going? Their conclusions also followed the same pattern: If Hawking is right and we do find a complete unified theory, we shall know the mind of God. What the reviewers couldn't know is that Hawking had almost robbed them of this conclusion. At the last stage of the writing process, Hawking admits that he almost cut the last sentence of the book, which said that we would know the mind of God. He was glad he didn't. "Had I done so, the sales might have been halved."[266]

By deciding not to cut the final sentence, Hawking demonstrated his keen sense of sales and marketing. He also recognized that "undoubtedly, the human interest story of how I have managed to be a theoretical physicist despite my disability has helped."[267] In his autobiography, Hawking explicitly addresses the accusation that his publisher shamelessly exploited his illness and that Hawking was complicit because he had allowed a photograph – which he himself described as "miserable"[268] – of him in a wheelchair set against a starry sky to be used on the book's front cover. He rejects this allegation outright and explains that his contract with the publisher gave him no control over the design of the cover. "I did, however, manage to persuade the publisher to use a better photograph on the British edition than the miserable and out-of-date photo used on the American edition. Bantam will not change the photo on the American cover, however, because it says that the American public now identifies that photo with the book."[269]

Unfortunately, his explanation does not entirely ring true. After all, if Hawking objected to the proposed cover, he would certainly have fought against it. Hawking's dealings with his former editor demonstrate that he was willing to threaten the complete cancellation of a book if his choice of cover was ignored. Whenever it came to negotiations with publishers, Hawking was known for being extremely assertive in getting his own way. It is worth noting that in his autobiography he does *not* attempt to claim that the publisher chose the cover against his will. And he never claims that he tried to dissuade the publisher from using the wheelchair photo on the cover. The only explanation he offers relates to the legalese in his publishing contract – a common feature of almost all publishing contracts that gave the publisher the final say on the design of the book's cover.

Hawking's editor also commented on the accusations that the wheelchair photo on the cover in any way took advantage of Hawking. "It was obvious the reviewer didn't know Stephen, to think that he could be exploited. No one could exploit Stephen Hawking. He is quite capable of looking after himself." On another occasion, the editor commented, "It was a triumph for a man in Hawking's physical condition to be on the cover of his own book."[270]

Hawking also refutes the suggestion that many people bought the book without actually ever reading it. He refers to the piles of letters he received from readers, full of questions and detailed comments indicating "that they have read it, even if they do not understand all of it." He also mentions that strangers stopped him on the street to tell him how much they enjoyed the book. As a result, Hawking concluded "that at least a proportion of those who buy the book actually do read it."[271] Well, for a scientist of Hawking's stature, this line of argumentation is not exactly conclusive. Like every author, Hawking naturally wanted his books not only to be bought, but also to be read and understood. Above all, the entire story surrounding the publication and incredible success of Hawking's *Brief History of Time* provides ample confirmation of Hawking's exquisite feeling for self-marketing.

A majority of scientists do not write popular science books – and this applies all the more to mathematicians and physicists. Hawking's book did not become a bestseller by accident but because Hawking was willing to do anything and everything in his power to make it a success. He parted ways with his tried and trusted academic publisher and moved to a general interest publisher because he loved the idea of his book being available in airport bookstores all across America; he repeatedly rewrote the book, despite the difficulties this caused him; he cut anything from the book that might make it less accessible to a non-scientific audience; and he also accepted the cover, which put his disability center-stage and showed him in a wheelchair.

Hawking also made sure he was actively involved in the book's marketing campaign. Within the book trade, some were amazed that he was willing to talk to tabloid newspapers such as the *Sunday Mirror*.[272] Shortly after the British publication of *A Brief History of Time*, people began to stop Hawking on the street to proclaim their admiration, which Hawking reveled in.[273] "I am pleased a book on science competes with the memoirs of pop stars," he explained.[274]

A Brief History of Time was the first, and by far the most successful, of Hawking's books for non-scientific readers. He wrote or co-wrote a total of 12 popular science books – including a children's book he co-authored with his daughter. Many became bestsellers, but none could match the runaway success of his first mass-market book.[275]

The hype surrounding Hawking and the book also had a flip side. Several physicists said that Hawking was wrong to mix accepted and established scientific conclusions with his own controversial speculations without informing lay readers of the distinction between the two. Others said it was pretentious of him to end the book with potted biographies of Galileo, Newton and Einstein. They felt that Hawking, by implication, was being arrogant by elevating himself in such illustrious company.[276]

Hawking's tendency to integrate scientific conclusions with his own speculations and opinions, combined with his inclination to express his personal thoughts on topics of general interest, created the model of success for his later books. In *Brief Answers to the Big Questions*, for example, Hawking explores the following topics at some length:

- Is there a God?
- Is there other intelligent life in the universe?
- Is time travel possible?
- Will we survive on Earth?
- Should we colonize space?
- How do we shape the future?

His answers to many of these questions have very little to do with scientific conclusions. His argument that we will not be able to survive on Earth forever because, for example, an asteroid collision could eventually end life on our planet, is by no means new. In fact, it is more or less common knowledge. On the basis of the risks our planet faces, Hawking describes it as inevitable that the human race will need to colonize other heavenly bodies.

Hawking also speculates that some researchers will use genetic engineering to breed a race of "superhumans." As a result, Hawking predicts that there will be major political problems with the "unimproved" humans, who would no longer be able to compete. "Presumably, they will die out, or become unimportant. Instead, there will be a race of self-designing beings, who are improving themselves at an ever-increasing rate."[277] This blend of science and science fiction contributed significantly to Hawking's popularity – and got him and his books onto the front pages of newspapers and magazines all over the world.

Like Einstein, Hawking often weighed in on political topics, expressing opinions that were generally in line with the left-wing, environmentalist zeitgeist: "The Earth is becoming too small for us. Our physical resources are being drained at an alarming rate. We have presented our planet with the disastrous gift of climate change."[278]

Convinced that the threat of climate change was worsening, Hawking issued ever-diminishing timescales for the imminence of disaster. In 2016, he declared that a disaster to planet Earth was a near certainty within the next thousand or ten thousand years. In 2017, he warned that climate change could turn the earth into a fireball with a temperature of 250°C and sulfuric acid rain within the next 600 years. The following year, he slashed the countdown to just one century – the human race had no more than 100 years before it would need to colonize another planet.[279] As early as the 1990s, Hawking began to develop doomsday scenarios, although the focus of his apocalyptic warnings changed over the years – sometimes it was computer viruses or genetic engineering, then it was nuclear war or an asteroid collision before, finally, he settled on rogue artificial intelligence.

Hawking had never actually researched any of these topics, but when stark warnings are issued by the world's highest profile scientist, people tend to sit up and listen. It's the same reason people hang on every word of Hollywood stars and other celebrities. Given their fame and celebrity status, the media are happy to devote frequent and widespread coverage to almost everything they say and do, even though they do not have the expertise or knowledge to comment on specialized topics.

Hawking always came up with new marketing ideas to draw attention to his scientific theories. Other scientists might have turned their noses up at addressing topics such as time travel – and if they ever did, they would have done so in scientific articles in academic journals. But Hawking had different ideas. On June 28, 2009, he organized a party for time travelers in his college, Gonville & Caius in Cambridge, to show a film about time travel. The room was decorated with balloons and "Welcome, Time Travelers" banners. To make sure that only genuine time travelers would come, he decided to send out invitations after the party and announce it on his 2010 TV show. "On the day of the party, I sat in college hoping, but no one came. I was disappointed, but not surprised, because I had shown that if general relativity is correct and energy density is positive, time travel is not possible. I would have been delighted if one of my assumptions had turned out to be wrong."[280]

On another occasion he made headlines for a scientific wager with the physicist Kip Thorne. They bet on whether or not the Cygnus X-1 system contained a black hole. The wager itself was nothing unusual, but the prize certainly was. If Thorne won their bet, Hawking promised him a year's subscription to the men's magazine *Penthouse*. "In the years following the bet, the evidence for black holes became so strong that I conceded and gave Kip a subscription to *Penthouse*, much to the displeasure of his wife."[281]

Even when he was wrong, Hawking managed to stage the admission of a mistake as a major media appearance that increased his popularity. During a conference in 2003, his scientific adversary Leonard Susskind compared Hawking to a soldier lost in the jungle who does not yet realize that the war he has been fighting is over. This was an allusion to the dispute between the two physicists about the fate of information that falls into a black hole, a disagreement that had been rumbling on for more than 20 years. "By the following year, he [Hawking] was ready to make a pronouncement, widely heralded as likely to be a public about-face. With characteristic showmanship, Hawking let it be known that his proclamation would be forthcoming at a conference in Dublin, and the global media descended on the venue to the bemusement of many scientists." He essentially conceded that his scientific opponents had been right and presented the physicist with whom he had concluded a scientific wager with a baseball encyclopedia. However, given the fact that Hawking qualified his concession with a major "but," some of his colleagues adjudged his performance to be "puzzling at best, and at worst a stunt in which Hawking hijacked the conference to boost his media profile."[282] He might have been wrong with one of his theories, but his publicly staged admission once again confirms Hawking's genius as a self-marketer: he was able to transform a scientific error into a media event with him at the center.

Hawking became more and more a jet-setting media superstar. He no longer devoted a majority of his time to his scientific work, but to popular projects and appearances around the world. After 2000, he largely traveled by private jet and the amount of traveling he did was relentless. In 2007, he caused quite a stir by taking a zero gravity, parabolic flight that enabled him, a man who was otherwise confined to a wheelchair, to experience four minutes of weightlessness.[283] Countless appearances on popular television shows around the world established him as the most famous and instantly recognizable scientist on Earth – a status that also made him the perfect subject for numerous documentary films. His name appears in the titles of eight successful documentary films or series, including *Stephen Hawking: Master of the Universe*, which was broadcast in 2008. According to one of his biographers, Hawking "may not have been the greatest cosmologist since Einstein or even in the top rank of modern physicists," but "he created a publishing phenomenon, met with popes and presidents, and filled concert halls in the manner of a rock star. He travelled the world, experienced zero gravity and hot air balloon flights, guest-starred in the world's most popular television series and was portrayed on the silver screen by movie stars."[284] He was without a doubt a genius – a genius of self-promotion.

Tools Stephen Hawking used to build his brand:

1. Hawking decided to work in a field where there was not so much competition and where he could more easily generate attention. When he was starting out, the most talented physicists were all choosing elementary particle physics, but Hawking decided to go into cosmology and general relativity, two fields in which far fewer scientists were working.

2. Hawking turned a disadvantage – his disability – into an advantage. The cover of his biggest bestseller was adorned with a photograph of him in a wheelchair. He even copyrighted the signature sound of his synthetic voice. And when it came to self-publicity and dealing with the media, he placed the "human interest" side of his story front and center.

3. Hawking was not bothered if his colleagues envied him or accused him of playing to the "popular science" gallery. He wanted to be popular and made every effort to write a book about science that would be accessible to a general readership – he was determined to write a bestseller. When negotiating with potential publishers, he made it a condition that the book would be available in airport bookstores all across America.

4. Hawking recognized the massive importance of active public relations. He even gave interviews to tabloid newspapers and guest-starred in television series and films.

5. Hawking was by no means modest. He included potted biographies of Galileo, Newton and Einstein in one of his books and repeatedly gave the impression that he regarded himself as the equal of the most famous scientists in history. In an episode of *Star Trek: The Next Generation*, for example, he appeared in a poker game with Isaac Newton and Albert Einstein. And he always made a point of the fact that that he was born on the 300th anniversary of Galileo's death.

6. With a hefty dose of fantasy, Hawking developed attention-grabbing stories for the media. For example, he invited time travelers to a party, but only sent out invitations after the party had taken place to ensure that only real time travelers would attend. It goes without saying that he announced this fact on television. He made public wagers with other physicists, but generated the greatest attention with his unusual choice of prizes, including an annual subscription to *Penthouse*.

7. He turned defeats into public relations victories. Even when forced to admit that he had lost one of his scientific wagers, he staged his capitulation as a major media event and generated the greatest possible media attention.

CHAPTER FIVE

MUHAMMAD ALI:
I AM THE GREATEST!

(ZUMA Press, Inc. / Alamy Stock Photo)

He went from being the most hated to one of the most revered athletes in the United States – a national icon. Muhammad Ali was the most famous athlete of the twentieth century and undisputed heavyweight champion of the world three times. His achievements in boxing were truly exceptional, but they weren't the decisive factor behind his astounding popularity. Above all, Ali was a genius in the art of self-marketing.

Muhammad Ali – born Cassius Clay Jr. – was a major celebrity even before his first successful title fight against the reigning heavyweight champion of the world, Sonny Liston, in 1964. A year before his victory, *Time* magazine (which then had a circulation of ten million) devoted a full front page to Clay. *Time's* cover featured a drawing of Ali with his head raised in a cocky, challenging pose and his mouth open. Above Clay's head, a pair of boxing gloves held a volume of poetry – an allusion to his habit of writing short verses. The lead article inside the magazine declared: "Cassius Clay is Hercules, struggling through the twelve labors. He is Jason chasing the Golden Fleece. He is Galahad, Cyrano, D'Artagnan. When he scowls, strong men shudder, and when he smiles, women swoon. The mysteries of the universe are his Tinker Toys. He rattles the thunder and looses the lightning."[285] When the article appeared, Clay was at the outset of his career. But even then, he wanted the world to know that he was the greatest, the most beautiful, and that no one could or would ever beat him.

A detailed computer analysis of film recordings of Ali's fights revealed that he landed 61.4 percent of the punches he attempted during the first phase of his career, from 1960 to 1967. In the second phase of his career, from 1970 onward, he only landed 50 percent of attempted punches. The same analysis also compared the percentage of punches the leading fighters of the twentieth century landed compared to the percentage of punches landed by their opponents. On this measure, the highest ranked modern boxer was the welterweight Floyd Mayweather Jr., who scored an overall rating of plus 25.2 percentage points. Joe Frazier scored an impressive plus 18.9 percentage points. Muhammad Ali's plus/minus rating was far worse, at minus 1.7 percentage points. Even when other factors are included in the statistical analysis, such as the number of power punches landed, Ali fails to rank among the best heavyweights in boxing history.

His biographer, Jonathan Eig, provides an honest assessment: "By all these statistical measures, the man who called himself 'The Greatest' was below average for much of his career."[286] Eig also raises another interesting question: "Did judges award him rounds that he didn't deserve because he possessed a flashy style and seemed never to be hurt by his opponents' punches? Was he winning rounds because he was the great Muhammad Ali?"[287] Some of his victories were controversial. As we know from other sports, referees and judges are not always unimpressed by the fame and charisma of a superstar athlete. The real reason that he was in with a chance of a title fight was his self-marketing genius. "Had he been an ordinary fighter with a record of seventeen wins and no losses against less than top competition, Clay would not have been in contention for a shot at the title," explains Eig. But Clay was not like other boxers. His big mouth and his habit of accurately predicting in which round his opponents would fall to the canvas were as much a factor as his pretty face. But most importantly, Eig credits Ali's rapid rise to the fact that he "became a sophisticated pitchman during a new age in marketing."[288]

Going back to the years before he entered the ring, Clay didn't do well at school and had trouble reading and writing. In 1957, he took an IQ test and scored well below average. His high school diploma was nothing more than a "certificate of attendance," the lowest degree his school could grant.[289] He graduated 376th out of a graduating class of 391 in his year.[290] In the mental aptitude portion of the military qualifying examination, Ali failed on his first two attempts and only became eligible for the army when the minimum score was lowered as the Vietnam War expanded.[291] In 1990, at the age of 48, he even admitted that he had never read a book in his life.[292]

The only thing he liked about school was the audience it gave him. "Attracting attention, showmanship, I liked that the most," remembered Clay. "And pretty soon I was the popularest kid in school."[293]

It took him 20 to 30 minutes to read a newspaper article other people would manage in four or five minutes,[294] but he had an incredible talent for public relations and, even as a young man, he outlined his media strategy and his approach to dealing with individual newspapers and journalists in exquisite detail.[295]

Ali's ingenuity in dealing with the media is perfectly illustrated by the time, early in his career, when he tricked the world into believing that he regularly trained underwater. In 1961, *Sports Illustrated* assigned a photographer, Flip Schulke, to take pictures of Clay. At one point, Clay asked Schulke which other magazines he worked for. Clay was excited to hear that the photographer's pictures regularly appeared in *Life*, the highest circulation magazine in the United States at that time. Clay asked Schulke if he would photograph him for *Life*, but the photographer explained that he worked on assignment and would have to pitch the idea to his editors, who would most likely turn it down – this was, after all, still very early in Clay's career. But Clay didn't let up and asked Schulke about his other work. When the photographer revealed that he specialized in underwater photography, Clay told him a "secret": "I never told nobody this, but me and Angelo have a secret. Do you know why I'm the fastest heavyweight in the world? I'm the only heavyweight that trains underwater." Clay claimed that he worked out underwater for the same reason other athletes wear heavy shoes when they train. "Well, I get in the water up to my neck and I punch in the water, and when I get out of the water I'm lightning fast because there's no resistance."[296] Schulke was suspicious at first, but Clay offered to let Schulke attend and take pictures of one of his underwater training sessions exclusively for *Life*. Schulke pitched Clay's proposal to *Life*, who liked the idea of running an article on Clay's unconventional underwater training routine. Of course, Clay had made up the entire story, but the successful outcome of his tall tale, namely a portrait in the highest circulation magazine in the United States, confirmed the effectiveness of Clay's approach.

According to Neil Leifer, a sports photographer who frequently covered Ali and his fights, "Ali was a photographer's dream ... Ali knew how to pose. I think it was vanity that made him concentrate on the camera ... A photographer couldn't miss with Ali. He made your job a success just by showing up."[297] Dick Schaap, one of the most famous sports editors in the U.S. at the time, recalls that Clay granted more interviews "than anyone else in the history of the earth. I can't imagine a politician or show business figure who talked to as many people so many times for as long as he did."[298]

Mike Katz, a well-known sports journalist who regularly worked for *The New York Times*, did not believe "that there's been an athlete in history who gave as much of himself to the media as Ali. He liked attention: he thrived on it." Katz even added that if there were no people around, Ali would probably do everything he could to attract the attention of a cat. "But he also worked cooperatively with the media and understood it as well as anyone I've ever known." He made time for even the smallest media and news outlets. "Ali would spend as much time talking to a tenth-grader from the local high school newspaper as he would to the boxing writer for *The New York Times*," says Katz.[299]

And in the words of Ed Schuyler from one of America's leading news agencies, Associated Press, there had never been an elite athlete "who was more accessible to the media than Ali. His training camp was always open. You could cover him twenty-four hours a day ... Once he saw a microphone or if two or three of us were taking notes, it was like someone threw a switch and a light went on."[300]

Even in the earliest stages of his professional career, Clay began wearing white T-shirts with his name printed on them in red. Other boxers always wore their names on the back of their robes, but that was only on fight nights. "It may have been the first time an American athlete devised his own name-brand apparel for daily wear. Already, he was emerging as one of the most adept self-promoters in all of sport."[301]

Clay was always coming up with new publicity stunts. Long before his first title fight, he mocked up a newspaper in a shopping mall in New York's Times Square with a headline he dreamed up himself: "Cassius signs for Patterson fight." "Back home," Clay explained, "they'll believe it's real."[302] He was known for his boasting ("I am the Greatest") and self-aggrandizement, and once he appeared for a weigh-in with a strip of masking tape covering his mouth – a gag that made even his opponent smile.[303]

Before his first world championship title fight against Sonny Liston, Clay rode around in a red and white bus emblazoned with big signs reading "THE GREATEST," "WORLD'S MOST COLORFUL FIGHTER," and "SONNY LISTON WILL GO IN EIGHT."[304] One night, Clay phoned a few newspapers and radio stations, urging them to get over to Sonny Liston's house if they wanted a good story. At one o'clock in the morning, Clay took his bus to Liston's house, rolled up at the curb and taunted the heavyweight champion, announcing, "I'm going to whup you right now!"[305]

One of Clay's most famous PR stunts was predicting the exact round in which his opponents would fall to the canvas. No boxer before him had ever done this and it created great suspense for journalists and audiences alike. Early in his career, Clay also began to compose short verses, which would later become his trademark. For instance, he told a reporter:

"This guy must be done,

I'll stop him in one."[306]

In another of his early fights, Clay predicted that his opponent would fall in the sixth round. Critics were offended by the fact that Clay would sometimes coast for a full round just to fulfill his prediction.

Clay, however, "liked his new gimmick, liked the extra attention that came with his increasingly bold behavior, and he was convinced that publicity would help him get a quicker shot at the championship."[307] He became even more of a showman and turned predicting when his opponents would crash to the canvas into his USP: "I'm not the greatest. I'm the double greatest. Not only do I knock 'em out, I pick the round. I'm the boldest, the prettiest, the most superior, most scientific, most skillfullest fighter in the ring today. I'm the only fighter who goes from corner to corner and club to club debating with fans. I've received more publicity than any fighter in history. I talk to reporters till their fingers are sore."[308]

On the one hand, Clay came across as aggressive and extremely boastful; on the other his pronouncements were typically accompanied by a cheeky glint in his eye and a hefty dose of humor. That made him popular. Before his fight with Liston, for instance, he said: "I don't just want to be champion of the world, I'm gonna be champion of the whole universe. After I whup Sonny Liston, I'm gonna whup those little green men from Jupiter and Mars. And looking at them won't scare me none because they can't be no uglier than Sonny Liston."[309]

When it came to the pre-fight weigh-in with Liston – championship bout weigh-ins had always been pretty boring and routine affairs – Clay went totally crazy, ranting, raving and hammering around on the floor with an African walking stick. It took six strong men to forcibly restrain him, or so it seemed, so he wouldn't go after Liston during the weigh-in. Most observers thought Clay had lost control of himself, was emotionally unbalanced, and would crack up completely before he even entered the ring for the showdown with Liston. However, one reporter who was observing the events more closely noticed that this too was nothing more than a carefully staged show and that most of what was happening seemed to have been planned in advance.[310]

Just as Arnold Schwarzenegger would succeed in popularizing bodybuilding in the 1980s – first in the United States and then worldwide – Clay attracted global attention to the world of boxing in the 1960s. Yet he did not see himself primarily as an athlete, but even more so as a star in the entertainment business. Even early in his career, this was something he was well aware of. "I don't feel like I'm boxing anymore. It's show business."[311] According to his biographer Jonathan Eig, Clay was "the greatest self-promoter the pugilistic world had ever seen."[312]

In 1963, Ali did something else no fighter before him had ever done:

he released an album of monologues and poems devoted largely to his own greatness. "I am so great, I impress even myself. … It's hard to be modest when you're as great as I am. … They all must lose in the round I choose. … I'm a perfect role model for children: I'm good-looking, clean-living, cultured and modest."[313]

Many of the prominent personalities described in this book were perceived by the people who really knew them as pronounced narcissists who had never really achieved emotional maturity. This is also true of Clay. Jerry Izenberg, one of the most famous sports reporters in the United States at the time, observed: "He loves people in groups, and they might hold his interest individually for a short period of time. But most of his interaction with people is centered on himself – not in an ugly way, but in a childlike way."[314]

Among Ali's most distinctive trademarks – from the beginning to the end of his career – were the short poems and verses that he initially wrote himself. They belonged to him just as the verses and sayings of Albert Einstein or Karl Lagerfeld became integral to their brand image. In 1963, Bundini Brown joined Clay's entourage. Bundini saw himself as a writer and demonstrated a great talent for composing witty poems for Clay. It was Bundini who coined what would become Clay's most famous slogan, "Float like a butterfly, sting like a bee." With these words, Bundini encapsulated Clay's style so aptly that the phrase was soon being quoted everywhere. During his career, Clay probably repeated these very same words thousands of times.[315] Although it seemed that Clay came up with his slogans and verses on the spot, this was very rarely the case. As the essayist Wilfrid Sheed recalled, "I'd hoped he made up his funny lines as he went along, when in fact I discovered he had a formidable memory bank of them."[316]

Clay was a quick learner and picked up ideas from other sports stars. He once appeared on a radio show with Gorgeous George, the most famous professional wrestler of his day. His sport had made him very rich, but he invested much more time and energy in self-marketing than he did in competing in the ring. After the joint radio interview, Clay watched Gorgeous George wrestle in a sold-out arena. "I saw fifteen thousand people coming to see this man get beat," he said. "And his talking did it. I said, 'This is a gooood idea!'"[317]

Clay was deliberately provocative with his pronouncements and loud bragging, fully convinced that many spectators only attended his fights to see this cocky young black man "get his pretty face disfigured." Later in his career, Clay became an outspoken political activist, a vocal advocate of civil rights and a leading opponent of the Vietnam War. But in the early years of his boxing career, none of these issues mattered to him. The leaders of the civil rights movement in the United States were disappointed that Clay seemed to exhibit so little interest in their cause. They were even angry at his habit of using racist stereotypes in his disparaging remarks about other black boxers.[318] At this time, Clay seldom expressed any of his personal opinions on issues of politics or race.[319]

Nevertheless, he increasingly embraced the Nation of Islam, an association which – unlike the civil rights movement led by Martin Luther King Jr. – strictly rejected integration and opposed white racism with black racism. Today, Clay is regarded as a champion of African-American equality and integration, but this is not true. In fact, he held segregationist views of his own: "In the jungle, lions are with lions, and tigers with tigers, and redbirds stay with redbirds and bluebirds with bluebirds."[320] Clay believed that integration was a mistake, and that black and white people should live separately. He also believed that a worldwide alliance of non-whites would ultimately lead to victory over the Caucasian minority.[321]

The champion of African-American equality, Martin Luther King Jr., also criticized Clay: "When he joined the Black Muslims and started calling himself Cassius X he became a champion of segregation and that is what we are fighting against."[322] Clay even left Americans scratching their heads when he praised the segregationist views of the right-wing fringe politician George Wallace.[323]

Clay, who became a member of the Nation of Islam and changed his name to Muhammad Ali in March 1964,[324] had lots of opponents – both white and black. "Ali may have been the most widely disliked man in America in 1965," writes his biographer Jonathan Eig.[325]

Ali was famous for refusing to be drafted to the military and for his opposition to the war in Vietnam. His reasons for taking such a defiant step changed with time, a fact that did not increase Ali's credibility. On one occasion he explained that the United States is a Christian country and that his religion forbade him from fighting in a war on behalf of "non-believers": "We are not, according to the Holy Qur'an, to even as much as aid in passing a cup of water to the wounded. I mean, this is the Holy Qur'an."[326]

Ali's most famous statement in declaring himself a conscientious objector was "I ain't got no quarrel with them Viet Cong." This sentence was quoted and printed on T-shirts all over America – it became one of the most frequently cited statements Ali ever made. With these words, Ali aligned himself with the generation of anti-Vietnam War protesters around the world in the 1960s. For some he became a hero, but many Americans turned their backs on him, offended by his unpatriotic attitude. Arthur Daley from *The New York Times* called for a boycott of Ali and said that people should refuse to watch his fights in person or on TV. "Clay could have been the most popular of all champions. But he attached himself to a hate organization, and antagonized everyone with his boasting and his disdain for the decency of even low-grade patriotism."[327]

In 1965, the World Boxing Association and the New York State Athletic Commission suspended Ali's boxing license. Other boxing commissions followed suit and Ali was stripped of his world championship title.[328] In June 1967, he was sentenced to five years in prison for refusing to serve in the United States military, a sentence he never actually had to serve as it was revoked three years later.

Ali's conflict with the state was compounded by a dispute with the Nation of Islam, who were incensed when Ali declared that he wanted to return to boxing in order to earn some money. It was not entirely logical that the Nation of Islam's leader, Elijah Muhammad, should take offence at Ali's decision, however, because he had not only accepted Ali's sporting activities in the past, but his son also earned splendidly from them. Ali continued to profess his belief in the Nation of Islam, but Elijah Muhammad eventually suspended his membership.[329] In a statement issued on April 4, 1969, Elijah Muhammad put his signature to the following words: "Mr. Muhammad Ali shall not be recognized with us under the holy name Muhammad Ali. We will call him Cassius Clay. We take away the name of Allah from him until he proves himself worthy of that name."[330] Despite this pronouncement, Clay continued to call himself Muhammad Ali and also affirmed his loyalty to the Nation of Islam and his faith. If anything, the enforced three-year interruption of his boxing career (1967 to 1970) after he was stripped of his belt and boxing license actually proved to be positive for him, as historian Jim Jacobs stated, "In some ways, the exile from boxing was the best thing that could have happened to Ali." Before his enforced break from boxing, a substantial portion of the American public had turned on Ali, "And worse, they were getting tired of hearing what he was about." Ali's exile created the space for him to reconnect with the people. Ali even became a symbol to those who had never shown any interest in boxing before.[331]

Ali continued his public relations campaign even during his forced exile from the ring, but with a different approach. He traveled around the country giving speeches at a large number of events. "In a way," said Jacobs, "it was like a presidential candidate sowing the seeds for future caucuses and primaries."[332]

When Ali returned to the ring after a break of more than three years, the mood had swung in his favor. Despite his long exile from boxing, he received much higher fees and became the highest paid athlete in the world. For his fight against the world champion Joe Frazier, dubbed the "Fight of the Century," Ali received a guaranteed payment of $2.5 million, by far the highest payday a boxer had ever received and equivalent to more than $15 million dollars today.[333]

Before his legendary fight with Frazier, Ali resumed his old habit of predicting the outcome of the fight, but this time with a twist. As a new PR gag, he had come up with the following stunt: Ali announced that, five minutes before the bout and on live TV, he would remove a sheet of paper from a sealed envelope. The piece of paper would contain his prediction of the round in which he would knock Frazier out.[334]

In the run-up to their fight, Ali painted Frazier, who was also black, as the white man's hope. "He isolated Joe from the black community. He constantly equated Joe with the white power structure, and said things like, 'Any black person who's for Joe Frazier is a traitor.'" On a television talk show, Ali went as far as to say, "The only people rooting for Joe Frazier are white people in suits, Alabama sheriffs, and members of the Ku Klux Klan. I'm fighting for the little man in the ghetto."[335]

For the rest of his life, Joe Frazier was bitter about Ali's unfair propaganda. "Calling me an Uncle Tom; calling me the white man's champion. All that was phoniness to turn people against me. He was helping himself, not black people."[336] It was a tactic Ali employed not only in his fight against Frazier, but whenever he competed against black boxers.

On 30 October 1974, Ali fought George Foreman in Zaire – a fight that was to go down in the annals of boxing history as "The Rumble in the Jungle." Before the fight, Ali went on a PR tour of Zaire to win over the country's inhabitants. On the flight to Zaire, Ali's advisers explained that some of his attacks on Foreman might not go down as well in Africa as they would in the United States. The majority of the population of Zaire was Christian and very few among them would understand the term Uncle Tom, which Ali otherwise used to disparagingly refer to his black opponents. Ali thought for a moment and then asked who the people of Zaire hated. After it was explained to him that the people in the former Belgian colony would hate Belgians above all else, Ali knew what he had to do. On his arrival in Zaire he roared, "I am the Greatest," followed quickly by "George Foreman is a Belgian." Ali had already painted Foreman, a fellow black boxer, as the white man's hope. Now, within minutes of touching down in Zaire, he had branded Foreman a colonialist oppressor of the Congolese. At one point, he went even further and branded Foreman "the oppressor of all black nations."[337] Just as Steve Jobs styled the competition between Apple and IBM as a fight between good and evil,[338] Ali turned a fight between two black boxers into a fight against the alleged oppressor of all black nations. "If he wins, we're slaves for three hundred more years," claimed Ali in a pre-bout TV interview. "If I win, we're free."[339]

On some occasions, Ali totally misjudged the impact of his exaggerated statements. In particular, one of the remarks he made in the run-up to the Foreman fight got him in trouble: "All you boys who don't take me seriously, who think George Foreman is gonna whup me; when you get to Africa, Mobutu's people are gonna put you in a pot, cook you, and eat you." The country's dictator, Mobutu Sese Seko, who had put up a lot of money to bring the fight to Zaire, was understandably angry because he wanted to use the global spectacle to spread his name and that of his country. Two days after Clay's statement, Mobutu's foreign minister called Ali's managers to reprimand them and Ali. "Well, please tell Mr. Ali that we are not cannibals; we don't eat people. We're doing the fight to create trade and help our country, and Mr. Ali's remarks are damaging our image."[340] Ali won by a knockout in the eighth round and, in reclaiming the world championship, disproved the supposedly cast-iron rule that "champions never come back" – before him only Floyd Patterson had managed to do so.

Over the next few years, Ali increasingly toned down his political statements. Only rarely did he refer to whites – as he had previously done – as devils. And although he remained loyal to the Nation of Islam's leader, Elijah Muhammad, he did not talk about his devotion quite as often as before.[341]

He no longer visited college campuses to speak out against the Vietnam War and stopped making politically inflammatory statements. "He gave the impression of a man who, above all else, was glad to be a boxer again."[342] As the legendary football player Jim Brown once observed, "When Ali came back from exile, he became the darling of America, which was good for America because it brought black and white together. But the Ali that America ended up loving was not the Ali I loved most. I didn't feel the same way about him anymore, because the warrior I loved was gone. In a way, he became part of the establishment."[343]

Ali even went as far as to publicly retract his earlier statement about having no quarrel with the Viet Cong. Now, he declared that he stood by his decision to oppose the draft, but, "I wouldn't have said that thing about the Viet Cong. I would have handled the draft different. There wasn't any reason to make so many people mad."[344] He went on to repeat his expression of regret several times. He also qualified his earlier stance as a conscientious objector by declaring that he would fight if America was ever attacked.[345]

Ali, a hero to the left-wing students of the 1960s, now irked many of his former supporters with his public shows of support for the Republican presidential candidate, Ronald Reagan, who was an established hate figure among left-wingers.[346] Ali's reconciliation with America was confirmed when he received the Presidential Medal of Freedom, the country's highest civilian honor, from Republican President George W. Bush in 2005.[347]

Clearly it was not just Ali that had changed. The United States of America had changed too – Ali and the American zeitgeist had re-converged. Ali owed much of his sustained popularity to the fact that he not only rebelled against the mainstream, he also became part of the new mainstream. In the 1960s, Ali was a leading figure in the protest movement, a vocal advocate of civil rights and a fierce opponent of the Vietnam War. As a fighter for the cause of African Americans and against the Vietnam War, he was despised and admired in equal measure. But once these battles were fought and a new America emerged in the 70s and 80s, Ali found it easier to adapt to the zeitgeist and to reconcile with his country. And his country with him. "My fight in the boxing ring was only to make me popular," Ali admitted. "I never enjoyed boxing. I never enjoyed hurting people, knocking people down. But this world only recognizes power, wealth, and fame – according to their procedures."[348]

Tools Muhammad Ali used to build his brand:

1. Outrageous boastfulness: Even Donald Trump's bragging doesn't come close to Ali's self-aggrandizing statements ("I am the greatest," "I am the prettiest," etc.). He was well aware that many of the spectators who came to see his early fights only came because they wanted to see a cocky young black man "get his pretty face disfigured."

2. Tireless publicity work: Hardly any other athlete gave so many interviews or made themselves so accessible to the media from the outset of their sporting careers as Ali, who became famous even before his first world championship title fight.

3. Creative PR: To secure a photo spread in *Life* magazine, he invented a story about training underwater. Before his fights, he predicted the round in which he would knock his opponents out, thereby adding to the suspense surrounding the fight. He also transformed his pre-fight weigh-ins into media spectacles.

4. At the start of his boxing career, Ali turned poems and short verses into his USP: "Dance like a butterfly, sting like a bee."

5. Provocation: He was not afraid of polarizing opinion or provoking people by expressing his (political) opinions in public. His uncompromising honesty increased his popularity.

6. He styled his fights as battles in the war for black liberation. Even in bouts against other black boxers, he disparaged his opponents as Uncle Toms and "the white man's champion." Ahead of his fight with George Foreman, Ali declared "If he wins, we're slaves for three hundred more years. If I win, we're free."

7. He resisted the mainstream, but shaped the zeitgeist and adapted to changing attitudes and social mores, even at the risk of disappointing some of his fans.

CHAPTER SIX

DONALD TRUMP: TROPHY REAL ESTATE, TROPHY WOMEN, TROPHY PRESIDENCY

(WDC Photos / Alamy Stock Photo)

Donald Trump polarizes. Today, he is possibly the most hated man in the world. And yet, in November 2020, he still managed to win the votes of over 74.2 million Americans, increasing the total he achieved in the 2016 election. But his opponent, Joe Biden, scored 81.2 million votes, most of which were probably not votes for Biden, but votes against Trump.

Trump was polarizing long before he went into politics. Whatever he has done in his life, everything has played second fiddle to becoming even more famous. And, despite the fact that some of his companies lost a lot of money, he always knew how to market his name and parlay his fame into money. In many cases, he only "lent" his name to companies, so when they lost money, he continued to earn as a licensor. "Donald Trump," wrote his biographers Kranish and Fisher, "has lived by the credo that all attention, fawning or critical or somewhere in between, accrues to his benefit, that his personal image defines his brand, that he *is* his brand."[349]

Trump is unlike most rich people. In most cases, the wealthy do everything they can to shield their privacy. For many years, Karl and Theo Albrecht, the founders of the German supermarket chain Aldi, were the richest people in Germany. They made sure that they never appeared in even a single photograph and they almost never agreed to be interviewed. Their private lives were shrouded in mystery and they lived in complete isolation, like many other rich people. In contrast, Trump "was the rare billionaire who shunned privacy, who invited cameras to focus on the ego wall in his office. He flaunted his wealth, spent ostentatiously, worked the media to keep himself on the gossip pages and the business pages and the sports pages and the front pages."[350]

As his biographer Michael D'Antonio observed, "For decades, no one has made a more insistent claim on the nation's attention than this man."[351] As early as the 1980s, a survey by Gallup in the United States revealed that Trump was the seventh most admired man in the world – only the Pope, the Polish folk hero Lech Walesa and the four U.S. presidents still alive at the time ranked higher than Trump.[352]

It seems as if Trump is less bothered about *what* newspapers write about him and only really cares that they *do* write about him. The subjects are interchangeable – money, politics, women, etc. – and the tone of the reporting is also less important. His only real concern is that the reports are prominent. For decades he has started his day by looking through a bunch of newspaper clippings in which he is mentioned. Long before Trump became the 45th President of the United States, his trademarks were world-famous and instantly recognizable to almost every American. According to surveys, 96 percent of Americans knew his name.[353] The most important components of the Trump brand were and are:

Success: Trump is the embodiment of the American dream, to which all other points mentioned here are subordinate. Whether he was buying trophy properties, seducing beautiful women, scoring high TV ratings or becoming President of the United States: All this apparently confirms that the name Trump is synonymous with unlimited success. D'Antonio wrote, "No one in the world of business – not Bill Gates, Steve Jobs, or Warren Buffett – has been as famous as Trump for as long. First associated with high-profile real estate development in 1970s Manhattan, his name soon became synonymous with success defined by wealth and luxury."[354] That is why Trump could not and would not accept his election defeat in 2020. He would much rather propogate the myth of election fraud than admit that he had lost.

Money: While other multimillionaires and billionaires are often happy to escape the attention of magazines such as *Forbes*, which publish annual lists of the wealthiest people in America, Trump regularly contacted the magazines' editors to say that his fortune was bigger than they reported. In fact, Trump was in a constant battle with *Forbes*. "Our rule of thumb was to divide whatever [Trump] said by three,"[355] observed Harold Seneker of *Forbes*. In 1999, Trump said that the *Forbes* estimate of $1.6 billion was almost $3 billion too low. "We love Donald," explained the *Forbes* editors, "He returns our calls. He usually pays for lunch. He even estimates his own net worth ($4.5 billion). But no matter how hard we try, we just can't prove it."[356]

Trump always estimated his assets as being worth more than the figures that appeared in the annual rankings because he placed an extremely high financial value on the Trump brand. He once explained the difference between two contrasting assessments of his net worth, one of which was $6 billion and the other $3.5 billion, by citing the value of the Trump brand. According to Trump, his name was worth $2.5 billion at that time.[357] Although the name Trump did not appear in the Interbrand ranking of the world's most valuable brand names, Trump stated in a 2010 deposition that an independent evaluation set its value at $3 billion. This would have made his name the single most valuable item in his portfolio,[358] because none of his properties or other investments were worth as much. One can assume that Trump's undignified exit from the White House has significantly diminished the value of his brand.

Beautiful women: As a young and wealthy man, Trump was attractive to women, and he did everything to systematically cultivate the image that women were clamoring for him. Beautiful women at his side, including models and winners of beauty contests (which he organized himself), were proof of his success. "For many years, he would call columnists and ask for their assessment of his latest romantic conquest, preferably with a numerical rating on a 1-to-10 scale."[359]

Trump even used to call journalists under a false name (Miller or Barron) and pretended to be Trump's publicist. On one occasion, after Trump's separation from his second wife Marla Maples, he even called a journalist to tell them that his "boss" had a whole list of beautiful women to pick from for his next love interest. "Important, beautiful women call him all the time," said the alleged publicist "Miller." He listed several names, including Madonna. "He mentioned basically every hot woman in Hollywood," recalled the journalist.[360] "And Trump's alter ego boasted that in addition to living with Maples, Trump had 'three other girlfriends.'"[361]

In his book, *Think Big and Kick Ass in Business and Life*, Trump wrote: "Beautiful, famous, successful, married – I've had them all, secretly, the world's biggest names, but unlike Geraldo I don't talk about it. If I did, this book would sell 10 million copies (maybe it will anyway)."[362] He claimed his women were the world's most beautiful: "I have been able to date (screw) them all because I have something that many men do not have. I don't know what it is but women have always liked it."[363]

Polarization, brazen statements: Trump never tried to please everybody. His statements were often deliberately provocative because he knew that this would attract media attention. "One thing I've learned about the press," said Trump, "they're always hungry for a good story, and the more sensational the better ... The point is that if you are a little different, or a little outrageous, or if you do things that are bold or controversial, the press is going to write about you. I've always done things a little differently, I don't mind controversy, and my deals tend to be somewhat ambitious."[364]

This strategy contributed significantly to his election success in 2016. As the election campaign progressed, Trump's statements became ever more provocative and extreme because he was sure that this would generate huge amounts of press coverage. And he was right. No other candidate received as much media attention as Trump. The fact that the coverage was predominantly negative did not tarnish his appeal to his political base. Quite the contrary. For his fans, the critical reporting was proof that the "establishment" they hated so much was intent on blocking Trump's path to the White House. On the one hand, Trump was terribly upset about negative reports, but on the other he felt that they could be of use to him. After all, it was a lesson he had already learned as a real estate entrepreneur: "The funny thing is that even a critical story, which may be hurtful personally, can be very valuable to your business."[365]

He even saw the positive side of scandalous headlines about his divorce from his first wife Ivana. While his father complained that he would have a stroke because of the story and his children suffered greatly from it, Trump told *Newsweek* that the scandal was "great for business."[366]

Ignoring political correctness: Trump's image is based on the fact that he is willing to say what many others think but do not dare to say. In the United States, "political correctness" has played and continues to play a major role. Many people believe that they cannot speak freely on certain issues because, if they do, they will be branded as racists, sexists, islamophobes or homophobes. Trump's predecessor as President, Barack Obama, for example, even had to apologize for making a positive comment about the appearance of a female attorney general – such a compliment was not politically correct. Trump, on the other hand, has blatantly ignored the accepted rules of language and refused to recognize the taboos of political correctness – all of which his supporters have found liberating. Although Trump has frequently been caught out by fact-checkers, his followers describe him as honest because he always says what he thinks: "I could give an answer that's perfect and everything's fine and nobody would care about it, nobody would write about it, or I could give an honest answer, which becomes a big story … I think people are really tired of politically correct."[367]

Luxury: Trump has always enjoyed flaunting his luxury lifestyle. He has surrounded himself in gold, even though others might think it tacky. Although he personally did not care much for boating, he bought a large yacht for $29 million. He then had it redesigned to his taste for an extra $8 million. His remodeling included gold-plating the sinks and even the screws.[368]

What intellectuals and white-collar professionals find repulsive impresses many ordinary Americans. In particular, blue-collar workers and immigrants can't get enough of articles about Trump, reported journalist George Rush: "He embodied the American Dream to them. Excessive, conspicuous consumption is not a bad thing in New York to a lot of people. It's kind of comic what he was doing, I've always felt like Donald was in on the jokes. He knows he's over the top, but that's where he likes to live."[369]

Man of the people: Many seasoned political observers were amazed that members of the lower classes could so strongly identify with a billionaire. But these ordinary people see a much wider gap to intellectuals, who typically pepper their speech with ten-dollar words and are proud to regularly read broadsheets newspapers.

In reality, Trump's image is far more glamorous than his real lifestyle. The editor of one of Trump's books recalled that, "Trump had this urge to be a really big name, so he cultivated celebrity. But his lifestyle was surprisingly unglamorous. He's quite disciplined in some ways. Doesn't smoke, doesn't drink, lives above the store. He was not a big New York socialite, never was. He basically enjoyed going upstairs and watching the tube. What he was interested in was celebrity and his businesses – construction, real estate, gambling, wrestling, boxing."[370]

In many respects, Trump's lifestyle and interests mean he has far more in common with regular Americans than he does with members of the educated elite. He'd much rather watch boxing, wrestling and reality TV than immerse himself in high culture, read a book or go to the theater. Many working-class Americans want to stay true to their roots; they just want to do so with a lot more money. And this is exactly what Trump embodies, this billionaire who speaks their language and loves the same things they do – quite unlike the intellectuals who think they are better than everyone else because they read sophisticated literature or are interested in the arts. Trump has no interest in the subjects intellectuals obsess over. Conversely, he knows a huge amount about pop culture. When the actress Kristen Stewart had an affair, he wrote that she had "cheated on her boyfriend like a dog." He advised the singer Kate Perry to watch out for John Mayer because he "dates and tells." According to D'Antonio, "As a TV star, he understands the importance of keeping up with trends and fashion to remain 'relevant.'"[371] After all, Trump became famous not as a businessman or politician, but as a TV entertainer and presenter of reality shows such as *The Apprentice*.

Real estate: Even the type of real estate he built or bought was often chosen based on whether it could serve to build the Trump brand. While his father became wealthy by building well-appointed but practical apartments for middle-class families in Brooklyn, Trump was drawn to Manhattan and bought properties such as the Plaza Hotel at completely exorbitant prices, because the image of the building with its Renaissance facade was more important to him than the hotel's profitability. The New York Plaza is indeed a legend and is the only hotel in the United States to be listed on the National Register of Historic Places. The first entry in the noble hotel's guest book was "Mr. and Mrs. Alfred G. Vanderbilt and servant"; the hotel has served as the backdrop for countless films and television series. And that's why Trump wanted to own it, even though the investment did not make sense from a business perspective.

Trump himself admitted: "I can never justify the price I paid, no matter how successful the Plaza becomes."[372] His sole aim was to acquire a "trophy" that would further enhance his image. And he added: "What I have done, however, is give New York the opportunity to have a hotel that transcends all others! I am committed to making the Plaza New York's single great hotel, perhaps the greatest hotel in the world."[373] Closer inspection reveals the absurdity of his words: He was offering New York "the opportunity" to be the location of a luxury hotel that had long existed there – and the city should "have" the hotel, despite the fact that Trump had just become the owner.

No rational property investor would have paid such a high price as Trump did: "To make interest payments, the Plaza needed to fill all of its 814 rooms every night of the year at a rate of $500 – more than twice what the hotel was charging."[374] In fact, the hotel turned out to be a bad investment and Trump was forced to give almost half of it to his creditors, along with the right to sell the whole hotel, in return for a reduction of the unbearably high interest payments. It was not until later that investors were able to turn a profit by converting the 450 rooms with a view of Central Park and 5th Avenue into 150 condominiums and leaving only 348 rooms with less attractive views of 58th Street as a hotel. Just like the Plaza, Trump had problems with some of his other investments, which he had acquired at inflated prices for reasons of prestige.

He had more success with a series of properties which, although they did not belong to him at all, were emblazoned with the name "Trump" in gigantic, gold letters. He collected substantial licensing fees, which the owners paid him for the privilege of using the Trump name, allowing him to profit from the brand name he had built up despite filing bankruptcy for his companies six times. To outsiders, however, it seemed as if Trump himself owned or developed all of the real estate that bore his name – and sometimes he even cultivated this misleading impression himself.[375] This was an excellent business for him, because he earned money as a licensor even when his local partners ran into massive financial problems.[376]

Exaggerated self-praise: Trump has never been guilty of understatement. There are countless examples of him stating that he is the greatest and the best, better than anyone else in the world or in human history. Here are just a few:

"Nobody builds walls better than me."[377]

"Nobody has more respect for women than I do."[378]

"Nobody in the history of this country has ever known so much about infrastructure as Donald Trump."[379]

"There's nobody bigger or better at the military than I am."[380]

"I know more about ISIS [the Islamic State militant group] than the generals do. Believe me."[381]

"Nobody knows more about trade than me."[382]

"Nobody knows jobs like I do!"[383]

"There is nobody who understands the horror of nuclear more than me."[384]

"I think nobody knows more about taxes than I do, maybe in the history of the world."[385]

"Sorry losers and haters, but my IQ is one of the highest – and you all know it! Please don't feel so stupid or insecure, it's not your fault."[386]

Trump also once bragged, "I'm a first-class sort of person" and added, "I only go first class."[387]

And when he was confronted with criticism – in this case the criticism that he was a racist – he also always responded with superlatives: "When it comes to racism and racists, I am the least racist person there is."[388]

In the wake of the 2020 election, which he lost, he went as far as to claim that no president in the history of the United States had ever won such an overwhelming landslide victory – and many of his supporters believed him.

Trump explained the media philosophy behind his exaggerations as follows: "The final key to the way I promote is bravado. I play to people's fantasies. People may not always think big themselves, but they can still get very excited by those who do. That's why a little hyperbole never hurts. People want to believe that something is the biggest and the greatest and the most spectacular. I call it truthful hyperbole."[389]

Trump's description of his statements involving "a little hyperbole" is of course a euphemism – and has nothing to do with being truthful. However, he was obviously counting on the fact that although people would not take everything he said at face value, they would believe that "there must be a nugget of truth to it." Since almost everyone exaggerates from time to time, even if they don't go quite as far as Trump, they will tend to assume that such statements have a certain element of truth to them. In addition, weak people can identify with someone with the brazen courage to say the things they are thinking but would never dare say out loud.

Trump's competitors – other real estate developers – frequently made fun of him and were appalled by his showboating.[390] They knew for a fact that he was by no means the most important or biggest real estate investor in New York, let alone the United States, as he presented himself. But Trump wasn't all that bothered by how his competitors saw him, he was interested in something else entirely – drawing maximum attention.

Do things others turn their noses up at: Trump was prepared to use any means to generate headlines. He did things that would have been highly embarrassing for other entrepreneurs or politicians. For example, when his friend, the wrestling promoter Vince McMahon invited him to take part in a one-off WWE event, *The Battle of the Billionaires,* Trump jumped at the chance. Trump selected a wrestler, Bobby Lashley, who was 140 kilos of solid muscle, to represent him against McMahon's choice, a 180-kilo Samoan named Umaga. If Trump lost, McMahon would shave Trump's head in front of 82,000 screaming fans. For Trump, the event paid off extremely well, as he reports in his book *Think Big and Kick Ass in Business and Life*: "The *New York Times* did a major piece on the fact that it was so successful … The event generated a lot of buzz."[391]

Failure is integrated into the success story: Several Trump companies went bankrupt and by the early 1990s he was almost broke. In the end, it was the banks that stepped in and rescued him. Trump has never made a secret of these setbacks. In fact, he has integrated them into his success story. In doing so, he has appropriated elements from the classic heroic sagas in which the hero is forced to overcome seemingly insurmountable obstacles in pursuit of his ultimately even more impressive victory. As the Roman philosopher and orator Marcus Tullius Cicero famously observed, "The greater the difficulty, the greater the glory." In his book *Think Big and Kick Ass in Business and Life*, which he co-wrote with Bill Zanker, Trump confessed, "I almost lost everything in the early 90s, but I got through it all and survived and thrived."[392] One day he was walking along the street with his then wife Marla and pointed to a homeless man and said, "That beggar over there is worth $900 million more than I am ... Because I'm $900 million in debt, and at least he has money in his pocket."[393] He was going through hell at the time. "I have the greatest respect for people who have experienced adversity and then come back. I was one of those people in the early 90s. I went through a tough period and learned a lot about myself, and then I came back bigger and better and stronger."[394] In fact, even his bankruptcies became an integral part of the Trump brand, which in the eyes of his admirers embodies the American dream that anyone can achieve anything.

Following his election defeat in 2020, however, Trump did not stay true to this principle. Instead of admitting defeat and taking personal responsibility for his loss, he denied it and thereby made what was probably one of the biggest mistakes of his life.

To get his messages across, Trump has always used every available media – press, TV, lectures, social media, books, etc. The first time he appeared in the media, or so he claims, was as a freshman in a local newspaper report on a baseball game: "Trump Wins Game for NYMA." Later he remembered: "It felt good seeing my name in print. How many people are in print? Nobody's in print. It was the first time I was ever in the newspaper. I thought it was amazing."[395] His biographer D'Antonio wrote that this "first brush with fame" could be seen as the spark that "would eventually light all of Trump's life ... Fame also established Donald Trump was a special boy. His deep appreciation for the experience shows that he understood that a great many people wanted fame but almost all of them failed to achieve it."[396]

Although he hardly ever reads, he has published a number of books that others wrote for him. His role was to take care of the marketing and drum up publicity for these books. He always approached a book launch like a presidential election campaign and took out full-page newspaper ads to sell himself and his books.[397]

Trump's fame reached an entirely new level with the success of his television show *The Apprentice*. He now had his very own TV show and proved to be a nice little earner thanks to his 50 percent ownership stake as one of the show's producers. The show was basically little more than one long advertisement for the Trump empire and lifestyle. "I'm the largest real estate developer in New York," he said in the opening montage that contrasted Trump in his limousine with a homeless man on a park bench. "I own buildings all over the place. Model agencies, the Miss Universe pageant, jetliners, golf courses, casinos, and private resorts like Mar-a-Lago ... I've mastered the art of the deal and have turned the name Trump into the highest-quality brand."[398] Trump fronted the show for 14 seasons and established *The Apprentice* as one of the most successful franchises on American television. The show was a top-ten program from its very first season and attracted 30 million viewers to its final episode.[399] The show allowed Trump to come across a little more "human," as a "billionaire with a heart, at times playful and unexpectedly willing to change his mind."[400]

Trump parlayed the increased popularity of the show into hard cash. He expanded his licensing department to include products of every kind under the Trump name: from hotels to clothing, furnishings to eyewear, from a financial services provider to an airline and even mattresses. By 2016, Trump was receiving income from twenty-five different licensing deals.[401] If the products and companies he lent his name to were successful, Trump basked in the glory of those successes; if they failed, he emphasized that he had nothing to do with the products themselves and was only licensing his name to them.

Trump's success is also due to the fact that he always employed a multi-media strategy to increase his popularity. In addition to newspapers, television and books, this included lectures, such as his guest appearances at motivational seminars hosted by Tony Robbins, which earned Trump $100,000 each.[402]

When Trump decided to go into politics, he was not primarily motivated by a particular political stance or a commitment to a specific policy agenda. He had changed his mind too often on all sorts of issues, from tax policy to gun control and abortion. Between 1999 and 2012, he switched parties seven times.[403] His positions seemed to change as often as the weather. In the early 1990s, for example, he advocated reversing Ronald Reagan's tax cuts and raising the top tax rate to 50 or 60 percent.[404] In this case, he was advocating traditional left-wing policies of the kind more usually associated with George Soros, Warren Buffett and some other American billionaires. As a candidate to become the Reform Party's presidential nominee, he trumpeted a number of policies that were typically advocated by the political left: "In the amalgamation that was his platform, Trump included items from the left side of the political menu, including a big, onetime tax on the rich to trim the federal deficit, a policy to allow gay soldiers in the military, and universal employer-based health insurance with subsidies for the poor."[405]

So, while his convictions changed, his ability to market himself remained a constant. During the 2016 election campaign, he made better use of social media, especially Twitter, than any of his competitors. It was almost as if the short message service and Trump were made for each other. Twitter allowed him to bypass critical media and communicate directly with his fans, providing him with a platform for his short and provocative messages that is far more effective than a politician's usual press releases and interviews. And that is precisely why it hit Trump so hard when Twitter deleted his account in the last few weeks of his presidency – because they blamed Trump for inciting his supporters to storm the Capitol. Other social media platforms, such as Facebook and YouTube, quickly followed Twitter's lead.

The world has rarely, if ever, seen an entrepreneur or politician who has so consistently dedicated himself to PR and the pursuit of publicity above all else. When Trump's ex-wife Ivana was asked what she thought motivated her former husband, she found it difficult to answer. Finally, she said: "I think he wants to be noticed."[406]

For Trump everything plays second fiddle to being noticed – even his hairstyle is an unmistakable trademark that reflects his personality: it's certainly not pretty, but it's unmistakable and, above all, it is eye-catching. "Poke fun if you will, but the painstakingly constructed swoosh and the artificial glow of Trump's coiffure make him instantly recognizable," said his biographer D'Antonio, "Without it, he might stand in front of Trump Tower and escape notice. With it, he is mobbed. His hair has drawing power, even if he didn't set out, in the beginning, to cultivate a billboard atop his head."[407]

Although he has been very wealthy during certain phases of his life (though never quite as wealthy as he claimed) and eventually even reached the most powerful political position in the world, the office of the American president, his aspirations were never primarily focused on money or power. For him, money and power were never ends in themselves, but only means to strive for larger-than-life fame. It was only once the whole world started talking about Trump every day that he had truly achieved his goal.

Tools Donald Trump used to build his brand:

1. Polarization, provocation: Trump provoked again and again with brazen statements to get into the headlines. *That* the media write about him is more important to him than *what* they write.

2. Trump constantly fed the media with fresh headlines about his private life.

3. He positioned himself as a "winner" as opposed to a "loser." He confirmed his status as a winner with ostentatious shows of his success: wealth, beautiful women, luxury/gold. Even in real estate investments, he was often more interested in prestige than profitability (as in the case of the Plaza in Manhattan).

4. Hyperbole and extreme self-praise: Trump greatly over-exaggerates and hopes that his followers will believe that there must be "some truth to what he says," even if they do not take every word at face value and know that he can be flexible with the truth.

5. Trump deliberately ignores political correctness and is thus perceived by his followers as a courageous person who dares to speak truths that others shy away from.

6. Despite his wealth, he presents himself as a man of the people, interested in television shows, reality TV, betting, wrestling, boxing, etc., but not in literature or high culture.

7. In the past, he wove his failures into his heroic story and reinterpreted every set-back as proof of his ingenious ability to overcome even the worst crises and emerge from them stronger. This strategy worked well for him. At least it did until his 2020 election defeat, when he seemed to lose his ability to read the mood of the people.

8. He turned his hairstyle into an unmistakable, instantly recognizable visual trademark.

CHAPTER SEVEN

ARNOLD SCHWARZENEGGER:

BODYBUILDER, ACTOR, POLITICIAN – THE THREE CAREERS OF A PR GENIUS

(Archive PL / Alamy Stock Photo)

In 1993, a survey revealed that Arnold Schwarzenegger was the man most Americans wanted to talk to on a long-haul flight. The only person ahead of him was a woman – Oprah Winfrey – and lagging far behind were the then U.S. President Bill Clinton and the singer Madonna.[408]

"I didn't want to be like everyone else. I thought of myself as special and unique and not the average Hans or Franz," wrote Arnold Schwarzenegger in his autobiography *Total Recall*.[409] In his biography of the embodiment of the American dream from Styria, Austria, Marc Hujer observed: "He has always wanted to be different from everyone else, has never wanted to conform to the world around him, and therefore he creates an environment that adapts to him, not the other way around."[410]

Even as a young child, Arnold was really into sports, although he wasn't keen on team sports because they didn't allow him to stand out like he could in individual sports: "I disliked it when we won a game and I didn't get personal recognition."[411] He added: "The worst thing I can be is the same as everybody else. I hate that. That's why I went into bodybuilding in the first place. It was the idea of taking the risk by yourself rather than with a whole team."[412]

Everything he became, he became through public relations. In his autobiography, he explained: "Whenever I finished filming a movie, I felt my job was only half done. Every film had to be nurtured in the marketplace. You can have the greatest movie in the world, but if you don't get it out there, if people don't know about it, you have nothing. It's the same with poetry, with painting, with writing, with inventions."[413] Many great artists throughout history have failed to make money from their works because they did not understand the importance of PR and were not good salespeople. On one occasion, Schwarzenegger observed that artists such as Picasso, for example, were forced to produce a sketch or paint a plate as payment for a meal in a restaurant; today, these works are worth millions of dollars. "That wasn't going to happen to my movies. Same with bodybuilding, same with politics – no matter what I did in life, I was aware that you had to sell it."[414]

In his various careers, Schwarzenegger has achieved everything there is to achieve. The boy who came from humble beginnings in an Austrian village set out to become the most famous bodybuilder in the world – and he did. Seven times he was awarded the Mr. Olympia title, the highest distinction in bodybuilding. Later he set himself the goal of becoming one of the highest paid action stars in the world. He went on to become one of the best known and highest paid actors in Hollywood, overcoming the significant obstacles that stood between him and his goal. He was twice elected governor of California, one of the biggest economies in the world and he probably would have liked to become president of America, but this was never an option because he was not born in the United States.

At the age of ten, he reported, he was absolutely convinced that he was special and destined for greatness. "I knew I would be the best at something – although I didn't know what – and that it would make me famous."[415] A normal life of the kind his father wanted him to have was the worst thing he could have imagined. "With my desire and my drive," explained Schwarzenegger, "I definitely wasn't normal. Normal people can be happy with a regular life. I was different. I felt there was more to life than just plodding through an average existence."[416]

Austria was too provincial for him. His goal, even back then, was America. One day, he saw a picture of the bodybuilder Reg Park, who was also an actor. He set his heart on emulating Park and identified bodybuilding as his route into the movies: "They would be the thing that everyone in the world would know me for. Movies would bring money … and the best-looking girls, which was a very important aspect."[417] In contrast to many other boys with similar dreams, young Arnold dedicated his iron will to achieving these goals and they became his all-consuming passion.

Even as a teenager, he had a keen sense for unusual methods of self-marketing – ably assisted by his mentor Albert Busek in Munich. One icy cold November day, Schwarzenegger took a stroll through downtown Munich wearing nothing more than a skimpy pair of posing briefs. Busek called a few editors he knew and asked them "You remember Schwarzenegger who won the stone-lifting contest? Well, now he's Mr. Universe, and he's at Stachus Square in his underwear."[418] The next day, his picture was in the newspaper. Schwarzenegger was depicted standing in his posing briefs on a construction site, flanked by a huddle of construction workers looking on in utter amazement.

Having emigrated to America at the age of 21, Schwarzenegger achieved his breakthrough with the help of his new mentor Joe Weider, who was the dominant figure in the world of North American bodybuilding. Weider had become wealthy by selling dietary supplements. He had, according to Schwarzenegger, "spun a whole myth about me: that I was this German machine, totally reliable, there's no malfunction, it always works. And he was going to apply his know-how and power to make this machine come to life and walk around like Frankenstein. I thought this was very funny. I didn't mind him thinking of me as his creation because I know that meant that Joe Weider would love me. This fit right in with my goal of becoming the world champion."[419]

Bodybuilding was then – even more so than today – a completely unknown sport, a "subcult of a subcult."[420] Unlike today, fitness studios were not ubiquitous features of every town and city around the world. "Muscle training," wrote Marc Hujer in his Schwarzenegger biography, "was then considered a sport for freaks, crazy men who wanted to have more bust than their girlfriends and who liked having thigh-sized upper arms. Bodybuilding is more like a circus act than a sport."[421]

Schwarzenegger won one championship after the other, but outside of the close-knit bodybuilding scene his victories were of no importance. Schwarzenegger, unlike many other bodybuilders, was not satisfied with this status quo. He made it his mission to popularize bodybuilding in America. "The more popular the sport became, the better my chances of becoming a leading man."[422]

In pursuit of his dreams, he employed strategies no-one else had ever thought of. Schwarzenegger developed a close relationship with a photographer, who succeeded in convincing the prestigious Whitney Museum of American Art in New York to host a live bodybuilding and art show, "Articulate Muscle: The Male Body in Art." On February 25, 1976, Schwarzenegger and two other bodybuilders posed on a revolving podium to the "visual accompaniment of slide-projected sculptures by Rodin and Michelangelo, while three thousand ticket-holders gawped in the gallery. The exhibition was the best-attended event the museum had ever staged ... *The New York Times* waxed enthusiastic."[423]

Schwarzenegger did everything he could to establish a close rapport with journalists – and not only with those who wrote for small circulation bodybuilding magazines, but with those who worked for magazines such as *Life*, where he could reach an audience of millions. His mentor Weider initially struggled with the new kind of attention,[424] but Schwarzenegger was determined to push bodybuilding out of the niche it was in. Bodybuilders, Schwarzenegger said, complained that reporters were always so negative about their sport and wrote stupid stories. "Well, that was true, but who was talking to the press? Had anyone ever sat down and explained what we were doing?"[425] Schwarzenegger was obsessed with PR. He once observed that, just as the three most important things in real estate are location, location, location, "Our motto was 'Presentation, presentation, presentation.'"[426]

Even at the outset of his career, Schwarzenegger already had an incredible feeling for PR. But he didn't rely on that alone. He hired professional public relations consultants. In her biography, Cookie

Lommel emphasized how important earning and retaining the public's respect was for Schwarzengger. In order to win it, he hired one of the top PR management teams in the U.S.[427]

Schwarzenegger became more and more famous and started getting invitations to appear on nationwide talk shows. He even benefited from the stereotype of bodybuilders as bone-headed musclemen, because his humorous manner and talent for entertainment allowed him to surprise people and win them over all the more easily. "The viewers were getting to see a bodybuilder who looked normal when he was dressed, who could talk, who had an interesting background and a story to tell. All of a sudden the sport had a face and a personality, which made people think, 'I didn't realize these guys are funny! This isn't weird, it's great!'"[428]

But even though Schwarzenegger's PR activities were gradually elevating bodybuilding from its niche existence, it was clear to him that bodybuilding would never allow him to achieve the popularity of a Hollywood actor. Moreover, he had already achieved everything that bodybuilding could offer. Therefore, he decided to start a second career as a movie actor. "I liked the idea of staying hungry in life and never staying in one place. When I was ten, I wanted to be good enough at something to be recognized in the world. Now I wanted to be good enough at something else to be recognized again, and even bigger than before."[429]

At first glance, everything seemed to be stacked against him. Again and again, Schwarzenegger was told that it was almost impossible for Europeans to gain a foothold in Hollywood. And this went double for someone with his physique, his strong Styrian accent when he spoke English and a name Americans couldn't even pronounce. "Forget it," he was told several times, "You've got a weird-looking body and you've got a weird-sounding accent and you'll never make it. Look, Arnold, you have very little chance in this profession because there is no one we know that has come from Europe – you know, from a German-speaking country or Italy or wherever – that has really gone through the roof, that has made it huge in this country."[430] This was indeed true, at least for male actors.

At best, producers and directors only saw Schwarzenegger as a muscleman, an actor who could take on small roles with little dialog in low-budget films. In his first – unsuccessful – film *Hercules in New York*, he spent the entire 90-minute running time flexing his muscles while the plot skittered dementedly around him.[431] The film flopped and is listed among the 100 worst films in history in the *International Movie Database*.[432] But, typical of Schwarzenegger, he was not discouraged by the film's failure.

His next two movies, *Pumping Iron* and *Stay Hungry*, also mainly focused on his body. But by this time, Schwarzenegger had already learned how to market a film. He built his self-marketing around provocative and striking statements which the media would happily quote over and over again. In *Pumping Iron*, he compared pumping up his muscles during training with an orgasm: "Blood is rushing into your muscles, that's what we call the pump. Your muscles get a really tight feeling, like you're going to explode … It's as satisfying to me as coming is; you know, as having sex with a woman and coming."[433] Later he explained, "To sell something on TV and stand out, I knew I'd have to do something spectacular, so I came up with comments like pumping up the muscles is much better than having sex."[434]

Schwarzenegger went all in on the PR for his films. He watched New York press agent Bobby Zarem very closely at work. "He taught me that ordinary press releases were a waste of time, especially if you were trying to get the attention of TV reporters."[435] Instead, Zarem contacted journalists personally and customized stories for each reporter. "Bobby was famous for his long, old-fashioned handwritten proposals. He let me read a four-page letter to the editor of *Time* explaining why the magazine should do a major story on bodybuilding … Bobby's job was promoting *Pumping Iron*, but I took a page from his book to get recognized."[436]

In his self-marketing, Schwarzenegger turned disadvantages into advantages. "By promoting *Pumping Iron* and bodybuilding, I was also promoting myself." People got used to his accent and his typical way of talking. "The effect was the opposite of what the Hollywood agents had warned. I was making my size, accent, and funny name into assets instead of peculiarities that put people off. Before long people were able to recognize me without seeing me, just by name or by the sound of my voice."[437]

Even after Schwarzenegger – together with a co-author – had written his first book, *Arnold: The Education of a Bodybuilder*, he insisted on unusually broad promotion and marketing strategies. "People won't buy this book unless we tell them it exists," he told his publisher. "Otherwise, how do they know? If you want to see it to go through the roof, then don't just send me to six cities. We're going to go to thirty cities, and we're going to do it in thirty days." The publisher was skeptical: "Thirty cities in thirty days! That's crazy!" Schwarzenegger replied that it was important to visit cities where stars normally don't ever go: "We can get more time on the morning shows that way."[438]

On a promotional tour for the book, Schwarzenegger had to take a flight from Atlanta to Birmingham, Alabama. He happened to observe a lively group of authors on their way to a literary seminar at the University of Alabama. Knowing someone in the group, Arnold asked what they were talking about, and his friend told him they were talking about literature, art and politics. "You mean they're not going to discuss how to sell their books?" asked the shocked Schwarzenegger. "They ought to invite me to that seminar. I'll teach those guys how to sell their books."[439] Schwarzenegger's biographer Andrews writes: "Marketing himself was becoming a major skill and obsession."[440]

For Schwarzenegger everything was subordinated to image building. "It's true, I am controlling about my image," he said. "If I'm not controlling my image, then who is? People always push things in the press; they want to be seen as a serious studio executive, as a smart businessman or as a sensitive artist. Politicians do it all the time; everyone tries to create an image of themselves."[441]

Schwarzenegger channeled all of his energy into his film career after leaving the world of bodybuilding, a career change that was designed to raise his profile exponentially. His strategy paid off with his first really high-profile movie, *Conan the Barbarian*. "It was different from being a bodybuilding champion. Millions of people were going to watch this move, whereas in bodybuilding the biggest live audience was five thousand and the biggest TV audience was one million to two million. This was *big*." Schwarzenegger recalled the excitement of knowing that "Magazines and newspapers around the world were going to review it."[442] He appeared "on as many national and local talk shows as would book me ... gave interviews to reporters from the biggest to the smallest magazines and newspapers."[443]

Schwarzenegger adopted a global perspective and emphasized time and again that "the world is your marketplace."[444] The studio's marketing people were planning to promote *Conan* internationally, not only in the United States, but also in Italy and France. *"Okaaay,"* answered Schwarzenegger, "but if you look at the globe, there are more countries than Italy and France … Why don't we be more systematic?" he asked. "Spend two days in Paris, two days in London, two days in Madrid, two days in Rome, and then go up north. Then say that we go to Copenhagen, and then to Stockholm, and then down to Berlin. What's wrong with that?"[445] In the end the studio agreed to let him promote *Conan* in five or six countries. "I felt that was a big step forward."[446]

When Schwarzenegger read scripts, he always evaluated them from a global perspective – in contrast to what was then common practice in Hollywood, which generated most of its grosses domestically. "Is this movie appealing to an international audience?" was always his first question. And even when it came to seemingly minor issues, he took a global perspective: "The Asian market is negative on facial hair, so why would I wear a beard in this role? Do I really want to forgo all that money?"[447]

Other actors and authors were reluctant to do PR, Schwarzenegger explained. The typical attitude was "I don't want to be a whore, I create; I don't want to shill. I'm not into the money thing at all."[448] Too many actors, authors and artists considered marketing beneath their dignity, according to Schwarzenegger. "But no matter what you do in life, selling is part of it."[449]

Schwarzenegger never wanted to be tied down to one role in his life – not as a bodybuilder nor as an action star in hyper-violent action films. He saw the chance to reach an even wider audience and gain even more sympathy by playing to one of his strengths – his humor. Humor had already become one of his trademarks in his action films. "Humor was what made me stand out from other action leads like Stallone, Eastwood and Norris. My characters were always a little tongue-in-cheek, and I always threw in funny one-liners."[450] These deadpan lines became his trademark and he felt that the dry humor somewhat softened the criticism that action movies were solely focused on violence. "It [humor] opened up the movie and made it appealing to more people."[451]

Schwarzenegger no longer wanted to be pigeonholed in the role of the muscle-bound action hero. Whenever he saw a comedy in the movie theater, he always thought: "I could have done that!" But nobody had ever offered him a comedic role. He decided that his next film would be a comedy.[452] For him this was the next logical step and would allow him to be perceived differently as a film actor, not just as *Conan* or the murderous cyborg in *The Terminator*. "I believe in systematically moving forward," said Schwarzenegger, "and not thinking that now I can do comedy because the studio will do it because I have power."[453]

He met with leading comedians and developed a real sense of humor and comedy timing. The comedy *Twins*, in which he starred as Danny de Vito's "twin brother," finally brought Arnold into the mainstream, broadened his acting repertoire and earned him more than any of his *Terminator* movies. In his autobiography he wrote that *Twins* had made him $35 million by 2012. A figure that is sure to have gone up by several million since then.[454]

Now that Schwarzenegger was an established Hollywood star, President George H. W. Bush appointed him as the nation's "fitness czar." If anything, Schwarzenegger's new role was nothing special. The president already had several czars who were supposed to champion different issues, but none of them had managed to attract much attention. This, however, is where Schwarzenegger's PR genius once again comes into play. He invested a great deal more energy into his role than anybody else would have done. "My own mission," he explained to President Bush, "should be to get out and promote." Bush was surprised when Schwarzenegger announced that he would travel to all 50 states to carry out his duties as fitness czar. "I love being on the road and meeting people and selling. That's what I do best."[455]

Normally, the White House press office would have sent out a short press release about the "fitness czar," and that would have been buried under the pile of many other reports landing in newsrooms across the country. However, Schwarzenegger suggested to Bush that the announcement should take place in the Oval Office. That, Schwarzenegger explained, would give the press an opportunity to take photographs and could be followed by a press conference during which Schwarzenegger could clarify his new role and the President could explain why Schwarzenegger was exactly the right man for the job.[456]

But even that wasn't enough. Schwarzenegger also suggested a large public fitness demonstration on the White House lawn. It was going to be a big celebration, "like Fourth of July," urged Schwarzenegger.[457] The event took place on May 1, 1990, was televised and the President arrived at exactly 7:19 a.m., because that was when the breakfast news ratings of *Today* and *Good Morning America* were highest. As Schwarzenegger observed, "Until then, I'd made dozens of appearances on morning TV and never paid any attention to what time I was scheduled to be on the air. But from then on, I would always insist on appearing sometime right around 7:30."[458]

For Schwarzenegger, PR was the right tool to solve any problem in any situation. After a heart operation, the number of scripts he was sent dried up because Hollywood executives doubted whether he was fit enough and because the insurance costs were too high. In this situation, he revved up his PR machine and made sure that pictures of him running on the beach, skiing and weightlifting got into the newspapers so that the whole world could see that he was back to his best again.[459] But Schwarzenegger had already decided what his next step would be. Early in his career, he had occasionally entertained the idea of going into politics. In an interview with the German news magazine *Stern* in 1977, he explained his plans: "Once you've conquered Hollywood, what could you set your sights on? Maybe power. Then you can switch to politics and become governor or president or something."[460] Of course, because he was not born in the United States, he could never have become president. But a recall against the governor of California gave him the opportunity to make the leap into politics.

Before taking a closer look at political issues, he thought about the right PR strategy: "We needed to avoid trying to win over the press and instead play to the people. When I went on TV, I'd go on entertaining national shows like Jay Leno, Oprah, David Letterman, Larry King and Chris Matthews rather than wonky local broadcasts. ... Above all, the campaign had to be *big*."[461]

He threw out the political rulebook by announcing his candidacy for the office of governor of California on the popular *Tonight Show*. Then, in order to head off questions about his economic competence, he recruited the renowned investor Warren Buffett to his team of advisors, despite the fact that Buffett is an avowed Democrat, while Schwarzenegger ran on the Republicans' ticket. He was determined to make it clear that he was not interested in traditional partisan politics.[462] Schwarzenegger repeatedly scored points in press conferences and talk shows with his humor and wit. At one press conference featuring Schwarzenegger and Buffett, a journalist asked: "Warren Buffett says that you should change Prop 13 and raise property taxes. What do you say about that?" Schwarzenegger answered, "First of all, I told Warren if he mentions Prop 13 one more time, he has to do five hundred sit-ups." So, he had the laughs on his side and Buffett, who didn't want to be a spoilsport, grinned. Schwarzenegger added that property taxes would not be increased under any circumstances.[463]

In television debates, he didn't adhere slavishly to one party's position and followed his campaign manager's advice to be himself, be likeable and have fun. "When things got especially intense, with everyone shouting over everyone else, I'd say something outrageous that would make the audience laugh."[464] American election campaigns can be dirty affairs. Opponents look for compromising details from every stage of a candidate's life, both professional and above all, private. Schwarzenegger was accused of sexually harassing women and making positive remarks about Adolf Hitler. With each of these accusations, he followed the basic rule: if the accusation was false, he denied it strenuously; if it was true, he accepted it and apologized if necessary.[465]

Schwarzenegger understood that a picture says more than a thousand words and used the power of images to communicate his core messages and attract attention. In Sacramento, he spoke to nearly 20,000 people in front of the capitol. He stood on the steps and gave a short speech, then a band played and he picked up a big broom. "That was the photo op: Schwarzenegger is here to clean house."[466] The photo went around the world.

He even named his California campaign bus "Running Man" (in reference to both one of his feature films and his current candidacy). On one campaign stop, he dropped a wrecking ball onto a car to symbolize what he would do to his opponent's vehicle registration fee if he were elected.[467]

In 2003, Schwarzenegger was elected governor of California by a large margin, and five years later he was re-elected. He showed an amazing ability to adapt, and when he misjudged the mood of the population, he was prepared to make radical course corrections. At the end of his autobiography, he summarized the most important rules of success and lessons life had taught him. One of these rules is: "No matter what you do in life, selling is part of it ... But you can do the finest work and if people don't know, you have nothing! In politics it's the same: no matter whether you're working on environmental policy or education or economic growth, the most important thing is to make people aware."[468]

The American magazine *Newsweek* once wrote, "Self-promotion comes as naturally to Schwarzenegger as flexing his triceps." And to the magazine *Cigar Aficionado*, the star explained "You have to let the world know what you have out there."[469] But for him, self-marketing was not only a means of achieving certain goals – building his brand was the prerequisite for freedom. "What I want," he said in an interview in 1977, "is to feel absolutely free. I want to be able to do absolutely anything for once, which means that I have to create a name and an image so that whatever I do is okay, and for that I need an incredibly powerful name – a name that everyone knows."[470] Throughout his life, "stay hungry" was always his motto – and this related above all to his hunger for recognition and fame: "Be hungry for success, hungry to make your mark, hungry to be seen and to be heard and to have an effect."[471]

Tools Schwarzenegger used to build his brand:

1. He chose bodybuilding as a niche sport where it was easier for him to become No. 1 – and then popularized it. He made his body his trademark.

2. In all his careers, the key to his success has been sales. His motto has always been, "No matter what you do in life, selling is part of it ... But you can do the finest work and if people don't know, you have nothing!"

3. In his film career he turned his supposed limitations – his unusual physique, his unpronounceable name and his accent – into his USP.

4. Catchy (sometimes provocative) statements and humorous one-liners became his trademark. He said that pumping his muscles was

like an orgasm. And he constantly used the catchphrases from his films ("I'll be back," "Hasta la vista, baby").

5. "The world is your marketplace": Schwarzenegger had a global outlook – unlike many Americans at the time. When it came to his films or his books, he organized international tours and visited as many cities as possible.

6. Schwarzenegger is a learning machine. He took other geniuses of self-marketing, especially Muhammad Ali, as his role models and learned as much as he could from them.

7. Although journalists did not take bodybuilding seriously and thought the sport as a whole was a bit of a joke, Schwarzenegger did not regard them as enemies. He took the time to explain patiently and with humor what the sport was all about.

8. He always sought to generate maximum publicity from everything he did. When the U.S. president appointed him as the nation's fitness czar, he was not content with a standard press release and turned the announcement into a huge media event.

CHAPTER EIGHT

OPRAH WINFREY:

THE AMERICAN DREAM COME TO LIFE

(wai yee thang / Alamy Stock Photo)

According to *Forbes*, **Oprah Winfrey** is one of the ten richest self-made women in America – and her name is certainly the most famous to appear in the illustrious top ten. *Life* hailed her "America's most powerful woman" and *Time* described her as one of the "most influential people of the century."[472] In 2003, Oprah made her first appearance on the *Forbes* list of billionaires – at that time there were only 476 billionaires in the entire world, and she was the first black self-made billionaire.[473] Today, she is estimated to be worth in the region of $2.7 billion and, in the United States at least, she has achieved a level of fame normally only enjoyed by the wives of presidents, including Hillary Clinton, who would most likely never have become a presidential candidate without her history as First Lady. No American woman has ever become as famous by their own efforts as Oprah.

Oprah Winfrey grew up in very modest circumstances – even if, as her biographer Kitty Kelly reports, Winfrey exaggerated her family's grinding poverty in the myth she subsequently created.[474] From a very early age, her goal was always to become famous. In junior high, when she was asked to fill in one of those "Where Will I Be in Twenty Years?" forms every young person is confronted with at some point, Oprah checked the box marked "Famous."[475] Many of the people who knew Oprah as a girl and young woman testify to the fact that she was always driven to become a star and be very rich.[476] For her, wealth was primarily a means of attracting attention. "In this society... nobody listens to you unless you have some bling, some money, some clout, some access."[477]

She discovered her talent for public speaking and started to make a name for herself by reading Bible texts in black churches around Nashville and by winning the Tennessee State Forensic Tournament.[478] She entered any competition that she thought would raise her profile and get her closer to the fame she dreamed of.

Having just won the Miss Fire Prevention competition, for example, she yelled out to the newspaper photographers crowding toward her to take her picture, "Here I am. Where's the camera? Here I am. Come see me."[479]

Oprah got her first break in television in 1974 – at the tender age of 20 – courtesy of a station in Nashville.[480] At the time, Nashville was the thirtieth largest TV market in the United States, so it made a great training ground for someone like Oprah, who was just starting out in the TV business. But her career really started to take off in 1976 with a television station in Baltimore. She was given the assignment of visiting a different Baltimore neighborhood each day to interview local people. Typical of Oprah, she judged her role primarily in terms of how it would increase her own popularity. As she explained to some reporters, "It's good PR for me. It was a great way of introducing me to the city."[481]

Oprah was soon promoted to co-anchor of the evening news, although she was clearly overwhelmed. She once read a report about a vote "in absentia" in California as if "Absentia" was the name of a town near San Francisco, because she had clearly never heard the Latin expression before. Her colleagues were very surprised when she started adding personal observations to news items, remarking at one point, "Wow, that's terrible." As one of her colleagues recalled, "From the start I knew it wouldn't work out. Oprah was just too inexperienced and limited in her knowledge of world affairs, especially geography, to be placed in [the] position ... of anchoring with the dean of Baltimore news [Jerry Turner]."[482] Unfortunately, she lost her prestigious position as co-anchor after just eight months.[483]

She was demoted to "weekend features reporter," which, by her own admission, was the lowest position in the newsroom hierarchy.[484] The "substantive" stories Oprah was now asked to report on included a cockatoo's birthday party at the local zoo.[485] But at least she was still part of the newsroom. When she was chosen as the host of a new morning show, *People Are Talking*, she felt she had finally reached rock-bottom. Her boss at the time recalled, "She really wanted to be a news person. She knew that news was all that mattered in television at the time. She saw daytime as a real come-down, a failure. She started crying. 'Please don't do this to me,' she begged. 'It's the lowest of the low.' ... What I was offering her was a real job and, quite frankly, she had no other option."[486] The station's general manager, Bill Baker, pulled out all the stops as he tried to make the new job more palatable, including a promise of a pay rise and a bigger production budget. She finally agreed, but left his office with tears in her eyes.[487]

It is a tribute to Oprah that she made the best of the situation, and in retrospect what seemed like a demotion proved a great opportunity to further her career. *People Are Talking* launched on August 14, 1978, and having interviewed two actors from her favorite soap opera, *All My Children*, Oprah said she felt like she had finally found her place in television. "I came off the air, and I knew that was what I was supposed to do ... This is it. This is what I was born to do ... It just felt like breathing. It was the most natural process for me."[488] Unlike her co-host, Oprah was not overly concerned about cultivating a sober, highly professional image.[489] For some journalists, there is almost nothing more important than being highly regarded, especially by their peers. Oprah, in contrast, was primarily concerned with "connecting" with her viewers. One of the most important tips Oprah was ever given was to always ask the first thing that comes to mind, no matter what. And it is advice she always followed. On one show, for example, she asked conjoined twins what happens when one of them needs the bathroom during the night. She was intrigued to know if the other twin has to go as well.[490]

Oprah embarked on the next stage of her career in 1983 when she started working in Chicago, the third largest TV market in the United States. Almost from the moment she launched her new show in Chicago, she was ever-present in the local media with a seemingly endless series of interviews. In late 1985, the *Chicago Tribune* described Winfrey as "the city's most over-celebrated celebrity."[491] Her self-congratulatory statements rivaled even Muhammad Ali or Donald Trump. For example, in one interview she explained, "I'm very strong ... very strong. I know there is nothing you or anybody can tell me that I don't already know. I have this inner spirit that directs and guides me ... I really like me, I really do. I'd like to know me, if I weren't me."[492] It was then that the national media started running features on Oprah. And because her show was so successful, it was soon picked up for national syndication. With more than 100 stations across the United States signed up to run her show, she received her first ever signing bonus, of $1 million.[493]

She was soon so well-known that she was cast in Steven Spielberg's *The Color Purple*, even if only in a supporting role. Although the film and its actors were nominated for eleven Oscars, they ultimately went home empty handed, having missed out on all of the coveted awards.[494] Winfrey was angry with Spielberg because he had refused to put her name in big letters on theater marquees or her face on the film's posters. To everyone but Oprah, Spielberg's refusal was quite understandable. It certainly would have been unusual to give so much publicity to a supporting actress who wasn't even that well-known at the time.[495]

But her film role, combined with the national syndication of her show, gave her popularity an enormous boost. *People* magazine invited Oprah to appear on the cover of their January 1987 issue. Over the next two decades, she made the cover an incredible twelve times, just two covers shy of cinema legend Elizabeth Taylor.[496] According to *Variety* magazine, Winfrey earned more than $31 million in 1987, making her television's highest-paid talk show host. She was now earning even more than the veteran Johnny Carson, who was paid $20 million a year as host of *The Tonight Show*.[497] But Oprah was far from satisfied. She wanted to produce her own primetime show and sell it to the networks herself – just like Bill Cosby.[498]

Her show drew its highest ratings whenever it covered raunchy, tabloid-style topics. In prudish America, sleazy subjects equaled high ratings. It's a lesson Oprah learned during her formative years as a talk show host and held to in later years. One show, for instance, was called "The Man with the Micro-Penis." On another occasion, she dedicated a show to "The thirty-minute orgasm."[499] There was no limit to her imagination when it came to sex-related subject matter: men who have been raped; women who have borne children by their own fathers; women abused during pregnancy; female teachers who had sex with schoolboys; a beauty queen who was raped by her husband, etc.[500]

She also invited members of a nudist colony onto her show. They sat naked onstage being interviewed by Oprah, with only their faces shown on television. Nevertheless, Oprah's viewers at home knew that she was interviewing a bunch of naked people in front of a studio audience, who were also getting a full-frontal view, and that was enough of a thrill to guarantee a ratings success.[501] On another show, she interviewed a woman who had not had a single orgasm during her eighteen-year marriage – together with the male sex surrogate who was giving her orgasm lessons. Next up were interviews with a sex-addicted woman who slept with 25 men in a single night[502] and three female porn stars, who shared graphic details of male ejaculations.[503] Housewife prostitutes, polygamy, sexy dressing and women who are allergic to their husbands[504] – Oprah never ran out of topics and her audience clearly could not get enough of them. But it wasn't all sleaze. Her audiences also responded enthusiastically to features on diet and relationship issues.

Another of Oprah's signature subjects was child sexual abuse. She made the national news when she interviewed a woman who talked about her experiences of being sexually abused as a child and Winfrey responded by revealing that the same thing had happened to her as a nine-year-old girl.[505] Oprah's family have always claimed that she invented this abuse – like many other things about her childhood and youth – to generate publicity for her show.[506] As is so often the case, it is practically impossible for an outsider to know who to believe.

Harvard Business School conducted a survey of the topics covered by Oprah's talk shows in the first six years since she went national. The survey found that she concentrated primarily on victims, "rape victims, families of kidnapping victims, victims of physical and emotional abuse, teenage victims of alcoholism, female victims of workaholism, obsessive love, and childhood wounds. She also covered therapy for husbands, wives, and mistresses; infidelity among travelling businessmen; and the worlds of UFOs, tarot cards, channelers, and other psychic phenomena."[507]

Andy Behrmann, a publicist who worked closely with the show, recalled, "For the most part her early years were devoted to tabloid sex trash that got huge ratings and shows about getting a man and keeping a man, and, of course, losing weight, because that's all she and her little cult really cared about. Unlike Phil Donahue, they didn't know anything about current affairs, politics, or the larger world around them, and they didn't care."[508] At the time of Oprah's arrival in Chicago, Phil Donahue was her biggest rival as a talk show host and many predicted that there was no way she could ever really compete with him. But the *Chicago Tribune* observed, "She [Winfrey] receives higher ratings with controversial shows on male impotence, women who mother their men, and guys who roll over after doing it, while Donahue tries to combat her with right-wing spokesmen and computer crimes."[509] As Winfrey's biographer Kitty Kelley reported, "Booking bigots, self-proclaimed porn addicts, and witches as guests gave Oprah, then thirty-four, soaring ratings over fifty-two-year-old Phil Donahue, whose talk show the writer David Halberstam once described as 'the most important graduate school in America,' informing millions about changes in society and modern mores."[510]

Oprah targeted a different audience to Donahue – the mass audience – and it was not all that interested in cerebral topics or international politics. While Donahue frequently interviewed politicians, including Jimmy Carter, Ronald Reagan and Bill Clinton, Oprah rejected high-brow interviews as a matter of principle because she regarded them as ratings killers. Instead, she managed to secure the kind of exclusives that eluded other talk show hosts – including a major interview with Michael Jackson, who had not given a live interview in 14 years. Winfrey sat down with the self-styled King of Pop at his Neverland Ranch and 90 million viewers tuned in across America for one of her finest hours of television.[511] With every celebrity interview, Oprah became even more of a celebrity herself.

Over time, the talk shows hosted by Donahue and Winfrey became, at least in some respects, more similar. Under pressure to deliver higher ratings, Donahue also started to focus on "tabloid" topics. "I don't want to die a hero," he said.[512] At the same time, Oprah's show was also shifting its primary focus. In 1989, she declared, "I used to be better sex and perfect orgasm. Then it was diet. The trend of the nineties is family and nurturing."[513] She started to present more shows on topics such as "How to Have a Happy Step Family" and "The Family Dinner Experiment."[514]

Later in her career, she reflected more critically on the kind of shows she had initially been so successful with and once admitted, "I've been guilty of doing trash TV and not even thinking it was trash."[515] Winfrey wanted to elevate her shows by focusing on more challenging features – including, for example, promoting books. In addition to audience ratings, image had now also become important to Oprah – she wanted to shed her reputation for doing "trash TV." But this change of subject matter carried the danger that she might lose her status as America's No.1 talk show host. After the Jerry Springer talk show outstripped her ratings in 46 of 47 weeks, Winfrey declared in frustration, "I'm introducing books and they've got penises."[516]

Oprah decided to reinvent herself as a motivational guru and launched what she called "Change Your Life" television in the late 1990s and totally redefined her role as a television host. "I am defined by the world as a talk show host, but I know that I am much more. I am spirit connected to greater spirit."[517] She positioned herself as the embodiment of the American dream, as a woman who overcame a difficult and abusive childhood and went on to craft an unprecedented career for herself and became the world's first black self-made billionaire. Tapping into her own life story, she motivated many millions of people – not only in America, but in all of the other countries where her show was broadcast. Simply put, people were inspired by her gospel: "If I can do it, you can do it."[518]

Left-wing, anti-capitalist critics, on the other hand, complained that success stories like Oprah's create the illusion that people can pull themselves up by their own bootstraps and work their way from humble beginnings to the very top through their own hard work: "During an era when people's actual power over the material condition of our lives has declined while the power of capital has expanded exponentially, Oprah Winfrey has ascended to the position of cultural icon of mainstream America by telling us we can do anything we put our minds to. This is a promise not unlike that of the lottery."[519]

Oprah, according to those left-wing critics, was just lucky. But

Oprah dismissed their claims: "Luck is a matter of preparation." She also made it crystal clear that, as she sees things, individual success has nothing to do with better or worse external conditions. "Anytime you look outside yourself for answers, you're looking in the wrong place."[520] She increasingly became an advocate for self-responsibility and success. Oprah's key messages included:

"Everything that happens to you, good and bad, you are attracting to yourself. It's something that I really have believed in for years, that the energy you put out into the world is always gonna be coming back to you."[521]

"It's what this show is all about, and has been for 21 years, taking responsibility for your life, knowing that every choice that you've made has led you to where you are right now. Well, the good news is that everybody has the power, no matter where you are in your life, to start changing today."[522]

"The message has always been the same: You are responsible for your life."[523]

Researchers became increasingly interested and conducted numerous scientific analyses of Oprah's talk show. One such researcher, Marianne Jeanette Crosby, conducted an in-depth content analysis of five shows from 1998 and five from the period between 2007 and 2009.[524] According to the analysis, one of the show's most frequently recurring "frames" was "Create your own Circumstances,"[525] which was one of the constant threads running through all of the analyzed talk shows. "The concept of this frame is that each human is in control of his own life and has full control of his current situation."[526] Oprah embraced and pushed the self-help philosophy of the book *The Secret* to her viewers. Thanks to Oprah's ringing endorsements, the book became a bestseller. In essence, Winfrey was telling every member of her audience that there was no real reason they couldn't, in her words, "get the job, the love, the life you want."[527]

Talk shows were just one of many vehicles Oprah used to position herself and expand her business empire. She appeared at countless personal growth seminars across the country and finally organized her own "Live Your Best Life" seminars, which attracted audiences in the thousands, primarily women.[528]

In April 2000, she launched *O, The Oprah Magazine*, which was a mixture of compelling stories, empowering ideas, gossip and personality cult. The magazine was a spectacular success and made her more popular than ever before. Within the first year, Oprah's magazine had a paid circulation of 2.5 million.[529] The magazine launched with Oprah on the cover, and that's how it would stay for the next nine years – she put herself on the cover of every single issue.[530]

All her life, Oprah had secretly dreamed of appearing on the cover of *Vogue*. However, when the idea was floated, the magazine's editor told Oprah, who was overweight for much of her life, that she would have to lose weight if she wanted to pose for the cover. Oprah promised to lose at least 20 pounds by the day of the photo shoot. She enrolled in a weight-loss boot camp, followed a strict diet and trained hard to make it onto the cover of *Vogue*. In October 1998, Oprah's *Vogue* cover hit the newsstands. It went on to sell 900,000 copies, more than any other issue in the magazine's 110-year history.[531] Her friend Stedman Graham explained just how much the *Vogue* cover meant to her: "It's like the culmination of all that she's worked for … From being overweight to this point is one of the greatest victories a person can have."[532]

Over the years, Winfrey has gone through repeated cycles of shedding pounds, only to put them all back on again. Like Karl Lagerfeld, Oprah shared the details of her weight loss and dieting with the public and launched a successful series of diet and fitness books. On one of her famous diets, she lost 67 pounds. In order to show her audience just how much that is, she pulled 67 pounds of greasy animal fat into the studio in a small red wagon. To drive the point home, she tried to lift the bag of wobbly fat. "Is this gross or what? It's amazing to me, I can't lift it, but I used to carry it around every day."[533]

The show was the most successful of Winfrey's talk show career – watched by 44% of the daytime television audience.[534] And when Oprah mentioned the secret of her dieting success, Optifast powder, a million viewers reached for their phones to bombard the company's toll-free order hotline.[535] The nation's media were transfixed by Oprah's weight loss for days – doctors, nutritionists and commentators all debated the merits of her diet.[536]

Following her diet, she declared that she would never gain weight again. But she had said the same thing so many times before and had eventually always put the weight back on. Her mostly female viewers sympathized as Oprah struggled with her weight, especially as so many of them had their own personal experience of this "yo-yo effect." Her viewers found it easier to identify with a frequently overweight woman who struggled with diets all her life than they did with a presenter with the figure of a supermodel. But whether she was moving up or down the scales, she always made her weight a topic of discussion on her shows and in numerous interviews.

In 1996, she published a book about fitness and dieting and it was an instant bestseller. It was also the springboard for her to launch an entirely new project: Oprah's Book Club. She wanted to get Americans reading, she explained, and her book club was a huge success. In the first year alone, the club sold almost 12 million books. According to industry analysts, she generated $130 million in book sales.[537] Oprah's Book Club skillfully combined all of her journalistic and entrepreneurial endeavors. She even used her talk show to endorse the books she had personally chosen. Publishers up and down the country were desperate to have their books discussed on her talk show. For them, there was almost no better guarantee that a title would storm to the top of the bestseller lists. In response to the overwhelming success of her book club, she received a host of awards and honors from publishing and library associations, and *Newsweek* dubbed her the most important person in the world of books and media.[538]

Winfrey's talk show was not just a sensation in the United States, it was broadcast in a total of 145 countries.[539] The vast majority of Oprah's viewers were and are women – according to a 2007 study, female viewers accounted for 73 to 78 percent of her total audience.[540]

Just like Donald Trump, Oprah Winfrey, despite her incredible fortune and fame, has always managed to create the impression that she not only has an affinity for ordinary people and their problems, but that she was in fact one of them.[541] And to a certain extent this is true. The problems Oprah had in her private life – especially her weight and diet issues, but also in her relationships – were the same problems so many of her viewers were also grappling with. "She is admired by women for her imperfect image and normal body. Also to many women, Oprah has been an inspiration to achieving personal goals and living a more healthy life," wrote Marianne Jeanette Crosby in an analysis of Oprah Winfrey and her talk shows.[542]

As Oprah became increasingly famous, a growing number of

acquaintances, both real and fake, contacted the media to sell scandalous stories about her eventful life. One of her ex-boyfriends threatened to expose the details of their past drug abuse – over a number of years, they had repeatedly taken cocaine and other drugs together. Oprah initially tried to kill these damaging stories, but soon realized how difficult that would be and decided to adopt a more aggressive PR strategy instead. She invited a drug addict onto her talk show and then – seemingly – spontaneously confessed that she had also been a drug addict.[543] This was an incredibly astute move. By publicly confessing her past problems with drugs, she defused the impact of the potential humiliation and robbed any such scandalous stories of their news value.

Having gained her first taste of acting in *The Color Purple*, Oprah openly declared that she did not just want to be a talk show host, she also dreamed of becoming a movie star. And she found what she hoped would be the perfect vehicle for her breakthrough in the film adaptation of the book *Beloved*, which was published in 1987 and earned its author, Toni Morrison, the first Nobel Prize for Literature for an African-American writer. The film, in which Winfrey played the leading role, was released in October 1998 with a gigantic, media-saturating, $30-million publicity campaign, not counting Winfrey's own widespread PR activities.[544] But the movie was a massive flop and destroyed her dream of joining the Hollywood elite. Rarely had a film been accompanied by such a huge marketing campaign, but in this case, Winfrey had let her own vanity get in the way. To many people, Oprah seemed to be promoting herself more than the movie or the serious subject behind the film – the terrible history of slavery in America. The fact that she spent so much time posing as a glamorous model in *Vogue* and on the covers of *TV Guide*, *Time*, *USA Weekend* and other magazines and extolling her weight loss did not really sit well with the film's important message. Whoopi Goldberg, who had starred with Winfrey in *The Color Purple*, was critical. "It's great to see that someone can create a frenzy the way Oprah has, but it's unfortunate it sort of backfired on the movie."[545] The high-profile director, Jonathan Demme, explained that despite the flop he would like to make another film with Winfrey, perhaps a comedy, "and we wouldn't hype it as much as *Beloved*."[546]

Oprah has always done everything within her power to shape her own image. She learned a painful lesson when she was humiliated by her drug-addict sister, who sold the story of Oprah's unwanted teenage pregnancy, drug abuse and other indiscretions to a tabloid newspaper. After this devastating experience, Oprah made almost everyone in her life – employees, talk show guests, interior designers, party planners, gardeners, pilots, bodyguards and even the vets who treated her dog[547] – sign a confidentiality agreement and forbade them from talking openly about Oprah's private life or business affairs.[548] The more powerful she became, the more control she exerted over the media's coverage of all things Oprah. In fact, she even frequently hand-picked which photographer would be allowed to take her pictures for newspaper articles.[549]

All celebrities care about their image, but rarely has anyone crafted their image as purposefully and consistently as Oprah Winfrey. She wanted control over media representations of her character, her appearance and her life story.

Tools Oprah Winfrey used to build her brand:

1. She never tried to beat her competitors – other talk show hosts – in areas where they were stronger, i.e. on political or cerebral topics. Even in the earliest phases of her career, she was indifferent when her critics accused her of being superficial and sensationalist. Ratings and popularity meant far more to her than critical acclaim.

2. Nevertheless, she constantly reinvented herself and managed to shed her image as the "Queen of Trash TV," for example by becoming the most influential authority for book endorsements as the founder of Oprah's Book Club.

3. Despite her undisputed celebrity status, Oprah always managed to make her audience believe that she was one of them. Her viewers felt that she understood them because she had the same problems and worries they did, including struggling with her figure and experiences of abusive or unhealthy relationships. For years, her talk show's theme tune was the song "I'm Every Woman."

4. She did everything in her power to control her image. For example, she banned her audience members from taking photos of her and even regularly dictated which photographers could take pictures of her for media outlets.

5. Although she regularly devoted her talk shows to topics that presented her guests as "victims," she still empowered people by giving them the strong hope that they could shape their own destinies and had the opportunity to change their lives and succeed, even if they had been victims in the past. If her audience needed further confirmation, Oprah's own life story offered the best proof: the rags-to-riches tale of a survivor of childhood abuse who went on to become the richest and most famous black woman in the world.

6. She never restricted herself to just one medium – television talk shows. She built an entire media empire spanning TV productions, films, magazines, a book club, the internet, lectures, and more. Unlike other journalists, she did not work as an employee for long; she built her own empire as a media entrepreneur.

CHAPTER NINE

STEVE JOBS:

THE ENTREPRENEUR AS ARTIST, REBEL AND GURU

(ZUMA Press, Inc. / Alamy Stock Photo)

There was hardly anyone who knew Steve Jobs as well as software engineer Andy Hertzfeld, a member of the original Apple development team. Steve Jobs, Hertzfeld reported, believed he was special, a chosen one. "He thinks there are a few people who are special – people like Einstein and Ghandi and the gurus he met in India – and he's one of them." Once, Jobs even hinted to Hertzfeld that he was enlightened.[550]

His biographers Brent Schlender and Rick Tetzeli wrote that Steve Jobs felt deeply entitled from the very start, "thanks to parents who raised him to think that he was every bit as special as they believed he could be."[551]

Jobs never saw himself as just a businessman. On several occasions, he stressed, "I never wanted to be a businessman, because all the businessmen I knew I didn't want to be like."[552] He saw himself primarily as an artist, a rebel and a guru. "As every day passes, the work fifty people are doing here is going to send a giant ripple through the universe." It was with words such as these that he motivated his team of developers.[553] He inspired his employees by instilling in them the idea that they weren't just working for any old company, designing and producing useful products for consumers, but that they were part of a greater mission.

The founder of Microsoft, Bill Gates, ended up as one of Jobs' fiercest rivals, although they did collaborate closely for a number of years. Gates once observed, "Steve was in ultimate pied piper mode, proclaiming how the Mac will change the world and overworking people like mad, with incredible tensions and complex personal relationships."[554] Trip Hawkins, former Apple marketing manager, was another to be impressed by Jobs' powers of persuasion and motivation. "Steve had an incredible ability to rally people towards some common cause by painting an incredibly glorious cosmic objective."[555]

During sessions with Jobs, Alvy Ray Smith, the co-founder of Pixar, was reminded of religious revival meetings. "I grew up a Southern Baptist, and we had revival meetings with mesmerizing but corrupt preachers. Steve's got it: the power of the tongue and the web of words that catches people up. We were aware of this when we had board meetings, so we developed signals – nose scratching or ear tugs – for when someone had been caught up in Steve's distortion field and he needed to be tugged back to reality."[556] According to Smith, Jobs, "was like a televangelist," enrapturing his followers.[557]

Jobs uttered one of his most legendary sentences in 1983, when he succeeded in convincing John Sculley, president of the Pepsi-Cola division of PepsiCo, to become Apple's new CEO. "Do you want to spend the rest of your life selling sugared water, or do you want a chance to change the world?"[558] Shortly after hiring his new CEO, Jobs invited Sculley and his wife for breakfast and confided, "We all have a short period of time on this earth. We probably only have the opportunity to do a few things really great and do them well. None of us has any idea how long we're going to be here, nor do I, but my feeling is I've got to accomplish a lot of these things while I'm young."[559]

Another programmer and early Apple employee was convinced by the words Jobs used to persuade him to join the company. "We are inventing the future. Think about surfing the front edge of a wave. It's really exhilarating. Now think about dog-paddling at the tail end of that wave. It wouldn't be anywhere near as much fun. Come down here and make a dent in the universe."[560] These are the kinds of words a guru would use, not a corporate leader. In fact, "make a dent in the universe" was one of Jobs' favorite go-to formulations. Another employee reported that Jobs repeatedly rallied his employees with sentences like these: "Let's make a dent in the universe. We'll make it so important that it will make a dent in the universe."[561]

Jobs never spoke like the CEO of a major company. He communicated like a visionary politician or the leader of a revolutionary movement. However, he was not planning on changing the world through politics, but with technology.

Jobs was temporarily forced out of his own company because he was so difficult to deal with in interpersonal relationships. When he eventually returned to the company he had founded, he described Apple's customers as follows: "The people who buy [Apple computers] do think different. They are the creative spirits in this world, and they're out to change the world. *We* make tools for those kinds of people … We too are going to think differently and serve the people who have been buying our products from the beginning. Because a lot of people think they're crazy, but in that craziness we see genius."[562] In a way, Apple employees were like members of a religious community or sect – Jobs was their guru and Apple's customers were following a vision that would change the world.

Jobs struck a chord, especially among young people. In a 2009 survey in the United States, twelve to seventeen-year-olds were asked to rank the entrepreneurs they most admired. Jobs topped the list with 35 percent of the vote, ahead of Oprah Winfrey and Mark Zuckerberg. When asked why they chose Jobs, nearly two-thirds of those surveyed gave responses along the lines of "because he made a difference," "he improved people's lives," or "he made the world a better place."[563]

Jobs' product launches were also legendary. According to his biographer Walter Isaacson, Jobs created a new kind of corporate theater. "The product debut as an epochal event, climaxed by a let-there-be-light moment in which the skies part, a light shines down, the angels sing, and a chorus of the chosen faithful sings 'Hallelujah!'"[564] His launches were as carefully designed and staged as theater productions. Jobs would stroll around the stage in his signature jeans and black turtleneck, sometimes holding a water bottle in his hand. On one occasion, Isaacson describes how "the crowd jumped to its feet, screaming as if the Beatles had reunited."[565]

Jobs positioned himself as a revolutionary and as an artist with a mission that went far beyond selling computers and smartphones. One of Jobs' most iconic product launches was the Macintosh computer in 1984. The Macintosh was not advertised as a new, attractive product, it was cast as a heroic warrior in the final battle between good (Apple and its followers) and the embodiment of evil (IBM). The ad featured a rebellious young woman on the run from the Orwellian thought police and throwing a sledgehammer at a big screen broadcasting a mind-controlling speech from Big Brother. Jobs styled his company's new computer (and its buyers) as resistance fighters, the last line of defense standing in the way of the big evil corporation's plan for world domination and total mind control.[566] In his product presentation, Jobs declared, "It is now 1984. It appears that IBM wants it all. Apple is perceived to be the only hope to offer IBM a run for its money. Dealers, after initially welcoming IBM with open arms, now fear an IBM-dominated and -controlled future and are turning back to Apple as the only force who can ensure their future freedom. IBM wants it all, and is aiming its guns at its last obstacle to industry control, Apple. Will Big Blue dominate the entire computer industry? The entire information age? Was George Orwell right?"[567]

Once again, this was not the kind of speech corporate leaders normally gave. This was far more the rallying cry of the leader of a revolution against a totalitarian state. Steve Jobs portrayed the competition between Apple and IBM as a struggle for "freedom" and against "mind control." And he clearly positioned himself as the self-styled leader of the rebellion. "Jobs," writes Walter Isaacson in his biography, "liked to see himself as an enlightened rebel pitted against evil empires, a Jedi warrior or Buddhist samurai fighting the forces of darkness. IBM was his perfect foil. He cleverly cast the upcoming battle not as a mere business competition, but as a spiritual struggle." Even thirty years later, Jobs still described IBM as "a force for evil."[568]

In *Presentation Secrets of Steve Jobs*, Carmine Gallo explains how Jobs established common villains that his audiences could rally against, not only in his famous 1984 product launch, but in every great presentation he ever made.[569] According to Gallo, Jobs was "a master at creating villains – the more treacherous, the better."[570] Like all gurus, Jobs always needed an enemy, even within his own company. He convinced his team that they were swashbuckling, rebellious pirates – while another team working on a different product at Apple was the equivalent of the navy. He and his team went to a retreat and one of his maxims was "It's better to be a pirate than to join the navy."[571] He even had the Jolly Roger pirate flag hoisted over the building where his development team were working on the new Mac.

Jobs was determined to position himself as a great designer and reap the acclaim for the design of his company's products. Jonathan "Jony" Ive, Apple's chief designer and one of Jobs' closest confidants, reported that Jobs often talked about ideas that came from Ive and his team as if Jobs himself had come up with them. Ive kept painstakingly detailed records of precisely who had come up with which idea first, and explained that "it hurts when he [Jobs] takes credit for one of my designs."[572]

In their biography of Jobs, Brent Schlender and Rick Tetzeli wrote that, "over the length of his career, he neglected to share credit for Apple's success in the press."[573] Whenever journalists asked to interview other Apple employees, Jobs always turned down their requests. He justified his stance by explaining that he did not want anyone to know who was doing the great work at Apple, because otherwise his best employees would be poached by other companies. Journalists saw through his protestations – they knew that "Silicon Valley was an incestuous place where tech talent was tracked as closely as the stock market."[574]

Jobs didn't want to share his fame with anyone or anything, not even his own products. Toward the end of 1982, Jobs was convinced that *Time* magazine was going to crown him their Man of the Year. But it wasn't Jobs who ended up on the cover of the magazine, it was "the Computer" that was chosen as the Machine of the Year. Inside the magazine, accompanying the main story, there was a profile of Jobs, which said, "With his smooth sales pitch and blind faith that would have been the envy of the early Christian martyrs, it is Steven Jobs, more than anyone, who kicked open the door and let the personal computer move in."[575] Jobs was devastated not to have been chosen for the *Time* cover. "They FedExed me the magazine, and I remember opening the package, thoroughly expecting to see my mug on the cover, and it was this computer-sculpture thing. I thought, 'Huh?'"[576] Jobs was so dismayed by the article and at not making the cover that he cried.[577] This incident illustrates the greatest difference between Jobs, the self-marketer extraordinaire, and his successor, Tim Cook, who once admitted, "Some people resent the fact that Steve gets credit for everything, but I've never given a rat's ass about that ... Frankly speaking, I'd prefer my name never be in the paper."[578]

Money was less important to Jobs than fame, explained his biographer Isaacson. "Instead his ego needs and personal drives led him to seek fulfilment by creating a legacy that would awe people. A dual legacy, actually: building innovative products and building a lasting company. He wanted to be in the pantheon with, indeed a notch above, people like Edwin Land, Bill Hewlett, and David Packard."[579]

The importance Jobs attached to his public image is reflected in the fact that he regarded money as little more than a tool to increase his own "visibility." According to his biographers Jeffrey S. Young and William L. Simon, Jobs was once asked about the effects of great wealth and named "visibility" as the principal factor. "There are tens of thousands of people who have a net worth of more than $1 million. There are thousands of people who are worth more than $10 million. But the number who have more than $100 million gets down to 100."[580] Through and through, Jobs was a marketing and public relations genius. Everything he did and said was in service of marketing himself and his products.

When Jobs returned to Apple in 1997, the company was in a desperate state. The stock price had collapsed, the company had no compelling products and the workforce was being downsized. Michael Dell, the billionaire founder of the eponymous PC business, was asked what he would do if he were put in charge of Apple, "I'd shut it down and give the money back to shareholders."[581]

It says a lot about Steve Jobs that his first move as Apple's CEO was to commission the same advertising agency that had been so successful with the "1984" ad to design a $100 million advertising campaign.[582] Even before he had any new, attractive products to launch, his strategy was to reaffirm his company's brand image with a campaign that didn't promote a specific product, but a philosophy. This ad campaign demonstrates just how strongly Jobs believed in the effectiveness of marketing and PR. The campaign was targeted not only at customers but also at Apple's employees, who were to be inspired to see themselves as part of a movement breaking with existing conventions. The theme of the campaign was "Think Different" and every print ad featured a black and white portrait of an iconic figure from history – Albert Einstein, Mahatma Gandhi, John Lennon, Bob Dylan, Pablo Picasso, the Dalai Lama, Thomas Edison, Charlie Chaplin, Martin Luther King, Jr. – along with less well-known figures. These were Jobs' role models, creative mavericks who had the courage to swim against the current, who succeeded in both resisting and shaping the zeitgeist.

The purpose of the campaign, Jobs said, was to remind people what Apple stood for. "We thought long and hard about how you tell somebody what you stand for, what your values are, and it occurred to us that if you don't know somebody very well, you can ask them, 'Who are your heroes?' You can learn a lot about people by hearing who their heroes are. So we said, 'Okay, we'll tell them who our heroes are.'"[583]

The original sixty-second version of the "Think Different" ad featured the following narration: "Here's to the crazy ones. The misfits. The rebels. The troublemakers. The round pegs in the square holes. The ones who see things differently. They're not fond of rules. And they have no respect for the status quo. You can quote them, disagree with them, glorify or vilify them. About the only thing you can't do is ignore them. Because they change things. They push the human race forward. And while some may see them as the crazy ones, we see genius. Because the people who are crazy enough to think they can change the world are the ones who do."[584]

Jobs referred to Apple – and thus to himself as the guru of the Apple movement – in the same breath as great historical figures, freedom fighters and artists because this is precisely how he saw himself, as an artist, not as an entrepreneur. Jobs was by no means a technological layman, but he did not understand technology to the same extent as his competitor Bill Gates or the co-founder of Apple, Steve Wozniak.

Even with his new company NeXT – which he founded in the period between resigning and returning to Apple – Jobs knew how to generate publicity and attract attention, despite the fact that the company didn't even have a product and was operating in a highly competitive industry.[585] The launch of Jobs' NeXT project also involved extravagant marketing and Jobs spent a fortune on a company logo before he even had a computer to market.

According to the early Apple engineer Andy Hertzfeld, "Jobs thought of himself as an artist, and he encouraged the design team to think of ourselves that way too."[586] He even took his team to a Tiffany glass exhibition to show them how great art could also be mass produced.[587] He repeatedly emphasized to his employees that he was aiming for the design of Apple's products to reach the quality of exhibits in the Museum of Modern Art.[588] When the design of the Macintosh computer had been finalized, Jobs summoned his team to a ceremony. "Real artists sign their work," he told them.[589] Jobs got out a piece of paper and a Sharpie pen and had each of them sign their names. Their signatures were engraved inside every single Macintosh. Bill Atkinson, one of the early Apple employees who developed graphics for the Macintosh, remembered, "With moments like this, he got us seeing our work as art."[590]

Jobs was fundamentally opposed to the prevailing view that design is nothing more than the outward appearance of a product or the quality of its packaging. For him, he explained in an interview with *Fortune*, "nothing could be further from the meaning of design. Design is the fundamental soul of a man-made creation that ends up expressing itself in successive outer layers."[591]

In conversations with his biographer Isaacson, Jobs articulated his legacy and emphasized the similarities between the world's greatest artists and engineers. Once again, he honed in on larger-than-life names, including artists such as Leonardo da Vinci and Michelangelo. Great artists and great engineers, Jobs explained, are similar in that they both have a desire to express themselves. "In the seventies, computers became a way for people to express their creativity. Great artists like Leonardo da Vinci and Michelangelo were also great at science."[592]

Jobs saw himself as an artist. He very consciously crafted and cultivated his own image. This began in his early youth. For example, he didn't say that he was adopted. "I didn't want anyone to know I had parents. I wanted to be like an orphan who had bummed around the country on trains and just arrived out of nowhere, with no roots, no connections, no background."[593] The role models Jobs learned from included people such as Robert Friedland, the steward of an apple farming community. Jobs watched as the charismatic Friedland made himself the center of attention. Jobs, who was still shy at the time, absorbed from Friedland how to sell and influence other people.[594] He learned how to stare at people without blinking and developed a technique for taking charge of situations – long silences followed by rapid bursts of fast talking. "This odd mix of intensity and aloofness, combined with his shoulder-length hair and straggly beard, gave him the aura of a crazed shaman," is Isaacson's description of Steve Jobs as a teenager.[595]

Because he considered himself to be special, Jobs always thought that rules should apply to other people but not to him. He drove his car without a license plate and regularly parked in disabled parking bays. Part of his self-stylization was his reputation for being able to achieve the "impossible," things that everyone else thought absolutely unrealistic and not feasible. If someone came to him with the word "impossible" or told him that something was simply not technically feasible, he was incensed. "If it could save a person's life, would you find a way to shave ten seconds off the boot time?" he asked one of his operating system engineers when they tried once again to explain to him why they could not accomplish something they initially dismissed as impossible.[596]

Adopting the same approach as he did with his products, Jobs also created unmistakable trademarks around his own image. At his product presentations he wore shorts, sneakers and a black turtleneck sweater. His sweaters were created by the famous designer Issey Miyake and he had about 100 of them made. On a trip to visit Sony in Japan, Jobs saw that employees wore a uniform and he was so excited about the idea that he called Miyake and asked him to design a uniform for Apple's employees. They hated the idea and, for once, Jobs did not get his way.[597]

Jobs gave fewer interviews to journalists than many of the other figures featured in this book. He focused entirely on his big product launches. He prepared them with an unparalleled level of perfectionism and they were reported on by all of the world's major media outlets. He was a true showman – he came to life on stage. For one thing, he could exert a level of control over events during his presentations that he could never achieve in a newspaper interview. At one of his earliest launch shows, Jobs paid a video projection company $60,000 to help out with the audiovisual presentation and hired postmodernist theater producer George Coates to stage the show.[598] The *Chicago Tribune* said that the launch "was to product demonstrations what Vatican II was to church meetings."[599]

According to his biography, "Jobs found ways to ignite blasts of publicity that were so powerful the frenzy would feed on itself, like a chain reaction. It was a phenomenon he would be able to replicate whenever there was a big product launch, from the Macintosh in 1984 to the iPad in 2010. Like a conjurer, he could pull off the trick over and over again, even after journalists had seen it happen a dozen times and knew how it was done. Some of the moves he had learned from Regis McKenna [his public relations consultant], who was a pro at cultivating and stroking prideful reporters. But Jobs had his own intuitive sense of how to stoke the excitement, manipulate the competitive instincts of journalists, and trade exclusive access for lavish treatment."[600] As standard practice, Jobs, who rarely spoke to the press, offered to provide "exclusive" interviews to selected media outlets as a quid pro quo for them promising to put the story on the cover.[601]

As a journalist, Brent Schlender accompanied both Bill Gates and Steve Jobs for many years. According to Schlender, Gates was usually very amenable when it came to taking photos. Gates' main concern seemed to be for the shoot to be over and done with as quickly as possible. When Schlender approached Jobs with a proposal for an article for *Fortune* magazine, the most intense negotiations were not about the article, but about the photographs that would accompany it. "Steve had all kinds of advice about the pictures that would accompany an article, especially about the stylistic approach to his cover portrait. He could be more than a little vain about how he was portrayed, and always sought the upper hand in deciding not only who would do the shooting, but *how* the portraits would be set up."[602] "Throughout his life," Schlender reported, "Steve had a keen sense of the tactical value of press coverage."[603] In fact, he was "more adept at managing the press than any other businessman alive."[604]

The art of successful public relations is all about communicating core messages and getting the media to do much of your marketing work for you. Jobs was an absolute master at creating specific, memorable soundbites. In his presentations, he worked with catchy, one-line descriptions and headlines that best described the product. For example, he introduced the MacBook Air with the simple headline "The world's thinnest notebook."[605] He knew that journalists love short, captivating headlines. Jobs had a headline for every product and they were carefully created in the earliest planning stages, well before a product was ready to be unveiled or marketed. For example, his headline, "The world's thinnest notebook" was repeated in every channel of communication at the market launch on January 15, 2008: presentations, website, press releases, interviews, advertisements, billboards and posters.

In *The Presentation Secrets of Steve Jobs*, Carmine Gallo described how the Apple founder used consistent messaging and carefully crafted headlines to communicate the vision behind his products. Jobs developed a short, clear message and repeated it at every opportunity. On January 9, 2007, for example, *PC World* published an article announcing that Apple would "Reinvent the Phone." But journalists at *PC World* did not come up with the headline themselves. Apple created it and Jobs repeated it five times during the keynote presentation in which he unveiled the iPhone. "Jobs does not wait for the media to create a headline. He writes it himself and repeats it several times in his presentation. Jobs delivers the headline before explaining the details of the product."[606]

Above all, Jobs was a marketing genius. He used the same principles he applied to marketing Apple products to establishing himself as a brand. In doing so, he did not play a fabricated role. The role he chose for himself was 100% authentic – with all his contradictions and craziness. Yes, he actually cultivated the craziness. His great weakness was his almost boundless lack of self-control in dealing with other people, whom he brutally attacked again and again. But he didn't try to hide this weakness, he made it a key component of the myth he created to portray himself to the outside world.

One journalist who knew Jobs well and even became a longstanding friend said: "Unlike most other CEOs I had interviewed for *Fortune* and the *Wall Street Journal*, Steve always seemed human and spontaneous with a penchant for honesty that stung and yet rung."[607] Jobs did not repress his feelings, he let them run free. He could cry just as unreservedly in the presence of others as he could shout and be goofy – and he often did both. But he could also be wildly enthusiastic, rousing others and winning them over to share his great visions. He detested normalcy and abhorred the idea of modifying his behavior to suit externally imposed conventions.

Social norms and rules do not apply to the rebel or the artist. In this respect, the creative type to which Jobs belonged is much like the entrepreneur as described by the Austrian economist Joseph Schumpeter. "Any deviating conduct by a member of a social group is condemned by the remaining members of the group" and this condemnation can potentially lead to the "social ostracism of the deviant individual."[608] This is why the majority conforms. Nevertheless, there will always be rare individuals who are incited by the shocked reactions of those around them and who "for this very reason behave with disregard for social norms."[609]

The person who wants to do something "new and unusual" not only has to reckon with external opposition "but also to overcome his own ingrained resistance."[610] The type of entrepreneur described by Schumpeter swims "against the stream."[611] In contrast to hedonistic, passive people, this type of entrepreneur struggles "against those 'bonds', a struggle to which not all are suited."[612] What's more, "The fact that something has not yet been done is irrelevant to him. He does not feel the inhibitions which otherwise constrain the behavior of economic agents."[613] This type "draws other conclusions from the data of the world around him than those drawn by the mass of static economic agents."[614] This entrepreneurial type is "quite indifferent to what his peers and superiors say about his business."[615] With these words, Schumpeter couldn't have described Steve Jobs better.

Tools Steve Jobs used to build his brand:

1. Rather than positioning himself as an entrepreneur, Jobs cultivated the image of an artist, rebel and guru. He gave the impression that more was at stake than just the latest electronic products, namely changing the world ("make a dent in the universe") and a struggle for freedom (Apple) and against total mind control (IBM).

2. Jobs elevated product presentations to an art form and made major launches feel more like religious revival meetings.

3. Jobs prioritized marketing and public relations. Having returned to Apple, but before he even had a new product to launch, he spent $100 million on the "Think Different" advertising campaign.

4. Jobs was a master of formulating bite-sized and quotable core messages for the media.

5. Jobs did not try to hide his weaknesses – he was highly emotional and frequently lost control of his feelings. He embraced them as components of his brand image. He could cry just as unreservedly in the presence of others as he could shout and be goofy. He celebrated his "craziness" and made it the core of his brand image.

6. Apple's corporate communication focused solely on Jobs. He exerted control over every aspect of the company's marketing and even insisted that he should have the final say on who photographed him for the media and how the portraits should be set up.

CHAPTER TEN

MADONNA:

I WON'T BE HAPPY UNTIL I'M AS FAMOUS AS GOD!

(Michael Bush / Alamy Stock Photo)

According to *Billboard's* **"Hot 100 Artists"** ranking, Madonna is the most successful female solo artist of all time and achieves second place in the overall ranking, just behind The Beatles.[616] In recognition of her influence beyond the world of music, *Time* included her in its "The 25 Most Powerful Women of the 20th Century" list.[617] She is one of the rare few female artists to be so successful over so many decades. In 2012 alone, the daughter of an Italian-American father and a French-Canadian mother earned over $300 million from a single world tour.[618] And as recently as 2016, Madonna was honored as *Billboard* magazine's "Woman of the Year."[619]

Experts agree that Madonna's extraordinary success has little to do with outstanding vocal abilities. Camille Barbone, Madonna's mentor and early manager, once observed, "Gifted? No. She was a meat-and-potatoes musician. She had just enough skill to write a song or play guitar. She had a wonderful sense of lyrics, however ... But more than anything, it was her personality and that she was a great performer."[620] Anthony Jackson, a respected session musician who played with a host of major stars, including Madonna, recalled, "I have to give Madonna a lot of credit. She knows she's not the greatest singer, but she knows how to get the music down. She's got style, and a way of choosing songs and guiding the way they go."[621]

In 1995, Madonna took on the lead role in *Evita*, the long gestating Hollywood film adaptation of the hit Tim Rice and Andrew Lloyd Webber musical from 1978. Even after she had landed the role, Webber remained unconvinced about Madonna's ability to sing the part. Madonna – at that time world-famous and at the height of her career – enlisted the esteemed voice coach Joan Lader to help develop her vocal technique.[622] Madonna was herself amazed at her incredible progress. "It was as if she had gone to bed and, magically, awoken a real *singer*," reveals her biographer J. Randy Taraborrelli.[623] Despite all of her hard work, Madonna fell apart when, on the very first day of filming, she had to sing "Don't Cry for Me, Argentina" in front of Andrew Lloyd Webber. She thought she had done a terrible job and ran from the studio with tears streaming down her face.[624] After an emergency meeting with Lloyd Webber and the film's director, Alan Parker, it was decided that Madonna should record her vocals in a smaller studio, away from the orchestra, which would record elsewhere. It was also decided that she would sing only every other day, allowing her extra time to rest her voice. Recording was a painstaking and extremely arduous process, with the cast and director working for four months before the soundtrack was complete.[625]

At the very beginning of her music career, Madonna's managers found it almost impossible to attract attention from record company executives who only heard her voice without seeing her light up a stage in person. "While her new managers were excited about Madonna's success on stage in front of live audiences, attempts to impress record executives with her demo tape did not go as well. Most people failed to be sold on Madonna's voice alone. She was a visual performer. The whole package was important, certainly not just the voice which was, at best, no more than average."[626] In 1991, Madonna explained, "I know I'm not the best singer or dancer in the world. I know that. But I'm not interested in that, either. I'm interested in pushing buttons."[627] And in 1999 she recalled, "Everyone agreed that I was sexy, but no one would agree that I had any talent, which really irritated me."[628] It is clear that vocal talent alone was not the reason for her remarkable career. And it is this fact that leads her biographer Taraborelli to ask at the beginning of his book, "What is it about this woman – an entertainer who isn't uncommonly beautiful and, while talented, is perhaps not phenomenally so – that has kept her on the top rung of the show-business ladder as the very symbol of success and glamour for more than thirty years?"[629]

The late 1980s marked the start of a new era in popular music, an age in which singers could become brands "and Madonna was one of the first to exploit this."[630] People who knew Madonna as a teenager all agreed "that Madonna had already made up her mind to be famous for doing *something*."[631] She knew that she wanted to become famous, but she did not know how or for what. Her friend Erica Bell remembers a conversation in which she asked Madonna what she most wanted from life. "I want to be famous," was her instant answer, "I want attention." When her friend said she was already getting a lot of attention, Madonna replied, "It's not enough. I want all of the attention in the world. I want everybody in the world to not only know me, but to love me, *love me, love me*."[632] In 2000, at a time when she was already incredibly famous, she admitted, "I have the same goal I've had since I was a little girl. I want to rule the world."[633] On another occasion, she confessed, "I won't be happy until I'm as famous as God."[634]

At first, Madonna never even entertained the idea of embarking on a career as a singer. She wanted to become a dancer and, in 1977, she won a scholarship to dance with the Alvin Ailey American Dream Dance Theater during a six-week summer workshop in New York. She was 19 years old and, for the first time in her life, she was surrounded by dancers as talented and ambitious as she was. "Everybody wanted to be a star," she recalled.[635] She was absolutely determined to become a leading dancer.[636] But she gave up contemporary dance when she realized that it would take years of backbreaking work to become a principal dancer or to establish herself as a successful choreographer and that it represented an extremely difficult route to becoming famous.[637] She even earned money for a while modelling nude for young artists. "And I thought it might give me a new thing, that maybe I might become a model. Who knows?"[638]

She later decided that acting would be her path to fame. She was constantly saying, "I want to be a movie star." One of her friends at the time says that, back then, music was little more than her ticket into the movies. "I don't think she ever thought she'd be doing music thirty years later."[639] But she later realized, "Music is the main vector of celebrity. When it's a success its impact is just as strong as a bullet hitting the target."[640]

Early on as a student, Madonna recognized a basic law of self-marketing: it is not solely or even primarily about being *better* than everyone else, it is important to be *different* from everyone else. Later in her career, she looked back and remembered, "Growing up in a suburb in the Midwest was all I needed to understand that the world was divided into two categories: people who followed the status quo und played it safe, and people who threw convention out the window and danced to the beat of a different drum. I hurled myself into the second category ..."[641] Even though she quickly discovered that this made her life significantly more difficult and earned her a reputation as a troublemaker, she realized early on, "I never wanted to do what everybody did. I thought it was cooler to not shave my legs or under my arms ... I dared people to like me and my nonconformity."[642] From the very beginning of her career in music, she wore unconventional clothing as a way to signal that she was special, that she was swimming against the tide. And she realized that by doing so she was able to attract the attention she wanted. She remembered her time as a dance student, "All these girls would come to class with black leotards and pink tights and their hair up in buns with little flowers in it. So I cut my hair really short and I'd grease it so it would be sticking up, and I'd rip my tights so there were runs all over them. Anything to stand out from them and say: 'I'm, not like you? Okay? I'm taking dance classes and everything but I'm not stuck here like you.'"[643]

Later in her career, she realized that provocation and violating social norms is one of the keys to building brand identity. "I'd rather be on people's minds than off," was Madonna's motto.[644] While other public figures are afraid of negative press, Madonna saw – much like Donald

Trump – that negative press could actually be positive and expand her fan base. "She believed that the more the press dubbed her style 'trashy,' the more vociferous the parental objection to her look, it would only encourage rebellious children to emulate her … Her success most certainly validated the blueprint for attention drawn up by Madonna as a child: do something to shock people and, if it's outrageous enough, it will get them talking. She didn't care what they were saying, as long as they were saying *something* about her."[645]

Madonna's public provocations mostly revolved around sex, including the frequent juxtaposition of sex and religion. In the video to one of her most successful songs "Like a Prayer," Madonna kisses a black Christ, is marked with stigmata, has tears of blood streaming down her face and dances in front of a field of burning candles. The video was relegated to late-night MTV and, when church leaders called for their congregations to boycott Pepsi, the soft drink giant swiftly pulled a big-budget TV commercial featuring Madonna.[646]

At the 1984 MTV Awards, the star writhed around and simulated sex on top of a massive white wedding cake. The host was bemused and many in the audience were outraged, but the press and photographers clamored to get a picture of Madonna after the show.[647] During her risqué stage shows, Madonna often simulated masturbation on stage. Once, during the North American leg of a world tour, Toronto police even threatened to arrest Madonna for obscenity if she went ahead with the show as planned. In response, she over-exaggerated the masturbation scene more than ever before, but the police decided not to intervene, despite their earlier threat.[648] There was also opposition in Italy, where Catholic pressure groups called for a boycott of Madonna's concerts.[649]

The excitement surrounding Madonna reached a climax in October 1992 when the singer published a 128-page book of erotic photographs and text bearing the provocative title *Sex*. The book was a showcase for Madonna's erotic fantasies, which were depicted in text and, far more frequently, photographs. In the book, Madonna explained why she was so into anal sex, while extensive photo spreads depicted her having sex with women. Above all, the book was a textual and visual expression of her affinity to S&M practices. Throughout the book, Madonna also appears engaged in scenes of masturbation. *Sex* was marketed as a limited-edition work of art and each copy was numbered. The manufacturing and printing processes were extremely elaborate and featured a spiral-bound metal cover, which was Madonna's idea. To underline the "forbidden" nature of the book, each copy was sold in a zipped silver foil wrapper.[650]

Reviews of *Sex* were generally negative. *The Washington Post* described it as "an oversized, overpriced coffee table book of hard-core sexual fantasies"[651] and *The Observer* branded it "the desperate confection of an aging scandal addict."[652] Despite the less than lukewarm reviews, the public controversy surrounding *Sex* catapulted the book to number 1 on *The New York Times* bestseller list.[653] A million copies of the book were published in seven countries on the same day, October 22, 1992, and immediately sold out.[654]

To coincide with the publication of *Sex*, Madonna also released a new CD, *Erotica*, accompanied by a video in which Madonna appears as a masked dominatrix. MTV refused to broadcast the video during the day and *Erotica* was the first Madonna CD to carry a warning on its cover: "Parental Advisory: Explicit Lyrics."[655] This time, Madonna's calculated strategy did not pay off and her continuous provocations were wearing thin. Disappointingly for Madonna, *Erotica* only sold two million copies.[656] In the wake of the controversy surrounding the publication of *Sex*, Madonna's popularity dipped to an all-time low.[657]

Whenever a figure in the public eye is subjected to an escalating stream of criticism, there is always a danger that the provocateur will respond by becoming even more radical and defiant. In Madonna's case, however, her PR genius comes to the fore and she knows precisely when to back down – or better still – to find a way back into her audience's hearts.[658] Toward the end of 1993, Madonna set off on a four-continent world tour, which she called "The Girlie Show." As her biographer Taraborrelli observed, "While still sexy, it was more of an innocent burlesque rather than a blatant attempt to shock. Gone were the hardcore S&M images and the blasphemous religious iconology of the previous two years."[659]

But that does not mean that Madonna was ready to entirely give up on being provocative. Her scandalous appearance on the much-watched *Late Show with David Letterman* on March 31, 1994, for example, was set to go down in history. Within seconds of the talk show beginning, Madonna called her host a "sick fuck" and unleashed a barrage of hostility at Letterman. "You used to be cool. Money's made you soft." In response to his efforts to calm the situation, she stepped up her attacks, "Can't we just break the rules? Fuck the tape, fuck the list. This is contrived." When Letterman tried to end the interview, Madonna refused to leave her chair. She was bristling with indignation. "Don't fuck with me, David. Don't make me act the fool." By the end of the interview, Madonna had used the word "fuck" a grand total of thirteen times, handed Letterman a pair of her underwear and talked about urinating in the shower.[660] The day after the show, Madonna was subjected to a no-holds-barred press onslaught and her popularity fell to another all-time low.[661]

Madonna returned to the familiar strategy of damage control. She knew that she had gone too far with Letterman and toned things down for her next talk show appearance on *The Tonight Show with Jay Leno*. She even publicly reconciled with Letterman at an MTV Awards ceremony.[662] Madonna realized that the controversy she inflamed with her shocking portrayals of sex and religion had become counterproductive. She took stock and decided that she no longer wanted to be associated with nothing but scandal. "So much controversy has swirled around my career this past decade that very little attention ever gets paid to my music," she now declared. "While I have no regrets regarding the choices I've made artistically, I've learned to appreciate the idea of doing things in a simpler way."[663] These are the words Madonna used to introduce her next studio album, *Something to Remember*, which was released in late 1995. According to one member of her management team, "She knew it was time to make a change. She would have to be pretty stupid not to know it, and you could never say that Madonna was stupid. She was upset, a little frantic about what people were saying about her. That's why she put together the 'Something to Remember' album, to remind people that there was more to her than just the controversy that had surrounded her almost from the beginning of her career."[664]

Moreover, Madonna was determined to finally make good on her dream of becoming a famous actress. Despite her success as a singer, she had never let go of this aspiration, which she had had since she was a teenager. Crushingly, her movie career had never really taken off and several of her movies had flopped, both with film critics and audiences alike. She saw her big chance when her name was linked with the lead role in the film adaptation of the musical *Evita*. She knew that she was by no means the first choice, but when it became clear that the original favorite, Michelle Pfeiffer, was out of the running, Madonna acted quickly and decisively. She sent a four-page, handwritten letter to the film's producer, director and screenwriter, Alan Parker, to explain why she was the perfect choice for the role of Evita. "In her letter, Madonna promised that she would sing, dance and act her heart out if Parker would only give her the opportunity to do so. She would put everything else in her life and career on hold in order to devote her time and energy to Evita."[665]

Madonna's letter is remarkable because it reveals another extremely important aspect of successful self-marketing. Other superstars – and Madonna was undoubtedly a global idol at the time – would have been too proud to write a four-page, hand-written petition of this kind. Madonna was undeniably very proud, but her pride took second place to her overwhelming desire to take the next step on the path to fame and to give her image, which had been battered by the controversy surrounding her perceived obsession with sex, a complete makeover.

However, having read the script for *Evita*, she was afraid that the film as written had the potential to damage her image because Evita – like Madonna – slept with so many men on her way to the top. She bluntly addressed her concerns with Parker:

"'It's just not me,' Madonna told director Alan Parker.
'Indeed, it's not,' he shot back. 'It's Evita Perón.'
'But my public will think it's me. And it's not.'
'But it's Evita Perón!'
And back and forth they went."[666]

Madonna was always highly conscious of her public image and pushed for changes to the script in order to portray Evita – and thus herself – as more human, more sympathetic and less calculating.[667] The film was released in December 1996 and – unlike most of Madonna's other films – it was a raging success, both at the box office and with critics. As with any drastic image change, Madonna's appearance in a mainstream musical disappointed some of her fans, especially those who loved her most for her rebellious and subversive nature.[668] But that was something she was prepared to live with.

At this point in her life, Madonna's priority was to recalibrate her public image. Her personal and artistic evolution was evident in her next album, *Ray of Light*, which she released in March 1998. "Without a trace of bondage or oral sex in a single lyric, this album's songs instead spoke of ecology, the universe, the earth, 'the stars in the sky,' angels and heaven and, surprising some observers, contained respectful references to God and 'the Gospel.'"[669] Madonna, who despite her 15 years of fame had only received one Grammy (for Best Video back in 1991), earned three Grammys for *Ray of Light* in 1999 – Best Pop Album, Best Dance Recording and Best Short Form Music Video.[670]

With this album, as with her earlier records, Madonna stamped her own identity onto emerging music trends, in this case embracing electronic and techno music, which she blended with her own musical style. She always understood the importance of constant reinvention, refusing to be pigeonholed to one fixed style or sound. This is a thread that runs throughout her entire career, beginning as early as her successful debut album. She was determined to try something completely different with her second album, an approach that made her record company, Warner Bros., extremely nervous. Her drummer Jimmy Bralower, who had previously worked with Chic and Hall & Oates, recalled, "When you have three hits in a certain vein, you do the same thing again. If it ain't broke, don't fix it. Madonna was bucking all normal trends, she was *fighting* trends."[671]

Her first album was heavily influenced by funk. Then came the shift to catchy, commercial pop songs in the vein of "Like a Virgin." As she matured as an artist, she increasingly incorporated elements from jazz or produced R&B/soul music with typical hip-hop elements. Later still, she integrated techno elements into her music.

Such constant reinvention requires a healthy dose of courage. At concerts, crowds repeatedly chanted for her to perform her catchiest hits, but Madonna only satisfied their demands to a limited extent. Her career is a balancing act between provocation and mainstream, between latching on to popular trends and avant-garde contempt for the all-too-comfortable. Accusations of "musical theft" have cropped up intermittently throughout her career, some of which even made it as far as the courts. Madonna absorbed influences from the musical world around her and was never afraid to copy from others.

Above all, she has always been willing to learn new things, and has never stood still for long. As Bill Meyers, the keyboardist in her live band, recalled, "At one point, she asked to do some vocal takedowns with me, her and the vocal coach. Some singers feel they don't have to do much, but she did."[672]

Her burning ambition drove her on and on. She wanted to improve herself continually. From the very beginning, Madonna was driven primarily by an overwhelming hunger to be famous. Even though she – like all celebrities – frequently complained about intrusive press coverage and the costs of fame,[673] she enjoyed being the center of attention more than almost anything else. Later in life, she even said that she refused to read newspaper articles about her,[674] but she only made such claims when she was in a funk because of a particularly inaccurate story. When the press coverage was positive, her reaction was quite different. In May 1985, for example, Madonna made the cover of *Time* for the first time. Madonna was waiting impatiently by the front door for the messenger to arrive with the envelope containing the first copy of the magazine bearing her image. She ripped the envelope apart to get to it and let out a shriek of unbridled excitement. "Oh my God, look at me!" Madonna cried out, dancing around the room in explosion of joy, magazine in hand. "I am on the cover of *Time* magazine! Can you believe it? Just look! Can you imagine it?" In response, her incredulous assistant declared, "No, I just can't believe it." Madonna suddenly stopped dancing and whipped around to confront her employee. "What do you mean, you can't believe it? Why shouldn't I be on the cover of *Time*?" Her assistant struggled to explain that she hadn't meant it like *that* and Madonna brought her anger to bear on her then boyfriend and later husband, the actor Sean Penn. She had her assistant call him to ask him to come over to her home to see the magazine for himself. When he told the assistant that he was too busy and she should send him a copy, Madonna grabbed the phone and, with an imperious edge to her voice, told him to get to hers straight away. "How many girlfriends have you had on the cover of *Time*? One! Me! Now, get over here."[675]

Sean, who was famous in his own right, hated the media hype around them and insisted that the marriage take place in private, but Madonna had her press agents alert the media without his knowledge, as she often did before they both went out for dinner or to a movie. Again and again, Sean was surprised that the press knew exactly where the two of them would be turning up. "What I don't understand is how the hell these guys know our every fucking move. Everywhere we go, there's a sea of fucking cameras!"[676] Madonna responded languidly, "We're stars, Sean. People take our picture. So, what's the big deal?" before adding, "Look,

I worked hard to get to a place where people care about me, and damn it, I'm going to enjoy every moment of it. So what? Get used to it or get the fuck out!"[677] One day, Penn fumed at her, she would have to choose between him or the media.[678]

Madonna invested a great deal of time and energy on generating publicity and developing her immense celebrity, but it was something she never liked to talk about. "Rather than have her public understand that a good deal of her immense celebrity had to do with her genius for public relations as well as her talent, it seemed that Madonna wanted the public to believe that it stemmed only from her talent."[679]

Just like Oprah Winfrey and Kim Kardashian, Madonna cultivated a huge female fanbase who saw far more in her than just a singer. Madonna presented herself as a modern feminist – not as someone who rejected or even hated men, but as a strong and sexually attractive woman who refused to conform to traditional expectations. Madonna defied categorization in almost every way possible and it was precisely her contradictions that made her such a popular figure and a mirror of the needs and desires of modern women. This effect was clearly seen in the book *I Dream of Madonna*, a collection of women's dreams about Madonna compiled by Texan folklorist Kay Turner. Here, women from a variety of ages and backgrounds described how Madonna the artist and singer figured in their lives. For some she was a liberator, for others a co-conspirator, an erotic seductress or an empowering enabler. "She has an everywoman quality, and what was remarkable at this time was the pervasiveness of her influence."[680]

Madonna's dream, in her own words, was to "stand for something." She knew that this was the essence of brand positioning. "I want to be a symbol of something. That's what I think when I think of conquering. It's that you stand for something. I mean, as far as I'm concerned, Marilyn Monroe conquered the world ... she stands for something."[681] For a host of women, Madonna was the embodiment of modern feminism that sees women as three-dimensional beings and rejects any idea of a contradiction between women's self-determination and the affirmation of sexuality and beauty. As the American feminist art and cultural historian Camille Paglia once wrote, "Madonna has taught young women to be fully female and sexual while still exercising total control over their lives."[682] According to Paglia, Madonna countered traditional feminism with a new brand of modern, popular feminism. "It was a startling appropriation of stereotypical feminist rhetoric by a superstar whose major achievement in cultural history was to overthrow the puritanical old guard of second-wave feminism and to liberate the long-silenced pro-sex, pro-beauty wing of feminism, which [thanks to her] swept to victory in the 1990s."[683]

For Madonna, feminism has never been about fighting men, but about taking all the liberties men have traditionally claimed for themselves – especially in sex. The older she got, the younger her lovers became. In 2019, at the age of 61, she made headlines for having a 25-year-old boyfriend.[684] These kinds of substantial age differences are usually the preserve of rich men, many of whom have much younger girlfriends. For Madonna, though, such behavior was an expression of a radical definition of freedom and living to the beat of her own drum. "I stand for freedom of expression, doing what you believe in, and going after your dreams."[685]

Tools Madonna used to build her brand:

1. She courted controversy with her depictions of sex (simulating masturbation on stage, S&M imagery in her *Sex* book) and by associating religious symbols such as the crucifix with sex.

2. She often pushed her provocations to the absolute limit, but when she realized that she had overstepped the mark and her popularity would suffer, she recalibrated her image and reverted to more conventional pop songs and stage shows – she returned to the warm embrace of the mainstream.

3. After a period in which she decided to focus exclusively on sexual themes, she succeeded in repositioning herself and redefining her image. She even demanded that the script of *Evita* be rewritten to better suit her new image.

4. She was not too proud to actively sell herself. Even as a world-famous singer, she seized the initiative and sent a four-page, handwritten letter to the producer of *Evita* to explain why she was perfect for the film's lead role.

5. Although she was not an extraordinary singer or dancer, and certainly not among the most talented actors of her generation, she still managed to establish herself as a leading performing artist and strong brand.

6. Madonna also positioned herself as a modern woman, who on the one hand saw herself as a feminist pioneer and on the other prized beauty and potent sexuality. She exploited her powerful sexuality and good looks confidently as her "erotic capital" without apologizing for it. For her, feminism does not mean fighting men, it means taking the same liberties as men – including having a lover 36 years her junior.

CHAPTER ELEVEN

PRINCESS DIANA:
QUEEN OF HEARTS

(parkerphotography / Alamy Stock Photo)

The life of **Diana** Spencer, who married the heir to the throne of England at the age of 20, demonstrates that even someone with little education and lacking in what would normally be described as high intelligence can become a master of self-marketing. For Diana, it was emotional intelligence, especially the ability to empathize, that enabled her to become one of the most famous and admired people in the world.

People with high emotional intelligence, in contrast to classic intellectual capacity, often demonstrate special empathetic abilities. They can sense what others feel, more quickly recognize the hidden signals in the behavior of others, and are more finely attuned to what others need or want. As early as 1983, the psychologist Howard Gardner suggested expanding the traditional concept of intelligence to include not only linguistic and mathematical skills, but also a range of other "intelligences." Emotional intelligence can play a far greater role in building oneself as a brand than the kinds of skills that are measured in traditional IQ tests. And a lack of academic education need not be a disadvantage. In fact, it can even be an advantage.

Diana was admitted to Riddlesworth Hall Boarding School at the age of nine and while her siblings flourished at school, she was considered to be an average student at best. She didn't leave school completely empty-handed, she did win the 'Most Popular Girl' trophy and the prize for the best-kept guinea pig. From 1973 she attended West Heath boarding school. The modest aims of the school were no secret and the only condition for admission was neat handwriting. But even at this boarding school, Diana's lack of intellectual curiosity was striking. "The groundwork wasn't there," said Ruth Rudge, the headmistress. "As with anyone with other things on their mind, she would go off in daydreams."[686]

Diana left her exclusive girls' boarding school, West Heath, at the tender age of 16, having failed every one of her exams not once but twice.[687] Diana's schoolmates remembered her fondly, describing her as a helpful person and "awfully sweet" to her two hamsters, Little Black Muff and Little Black Puff. As her biographer Tina Brown wrote: "Turning over examination papers turned her over inside ... She did, in fact, have a talent that West Heath had already noticed. She had a keen emotional intelligence."[688]

The historian and journalist Paul Johnson was once asked about Diana's empathy, which he regarded as a unique gift: "She thought she knew nothing and was very stupid," he said, "She made it impossible to criticize her, because she'd say 'I am very thick and uneducated,' and I'd say 'I don't think you are thick at all,' because, although she didn't know much, she had something that very few people possess. She had extraordinary intuition and could see people who were nice and warm to them and sympathize with them ... Very few people compare to what she had."[689] Even as the rich daughter of an earl, after Diana left school she worked as a nanny and cleaner.[690] She often made fun of herself for her lack of education. "Thick as a plank, that's me," she was often heard to shriek.[691]

After it became known that she was having an affair with Prince

Charles, an editorial in the British magazine, *Tatler*, asked doubtfully: "How will she react to the tumbling French Bourse after the election of Mitterrand when the topic looms over the egg mayonnaise? How will she cope with excited discussion about the justness of the Suss Law when it breaks over the lamb cutlets?"[692]

With her marriage to Prince Charles, she was elevated to the uppermost echelons of British society, where "Diana's intellectual inferiority complex kicked in with a vengeance."[693] While her husband was highly educated, read many books, was well versed in many fields and excelled intellectually in conversation, Diana became increasingly withdrawn, much to the displeasure of the Queen. Her Majesty was so displeased at Diana's silence during one dinner that she cornered a guest and exploded: "Look at her, sitting at the table glowering at us!"[694]

"Diana had keen emotional intelligence," writes her biographer, "but her lack of education meant she struggled with the framework of public affairs."[695] Diana's favorite books were romance novels by Barbara Cartland,[696] an extremely successful writer who wrote no less than 724 tear-jerking stories. By the end of Cartland's novels, the shy, inconspicuous heroine has usually won the heart and affections of a dashing prince or gallant gentleman. "In those stories," confessed Diana, "was everyone I dreamed of, everything I hoped for."[697]

Early on she dreamt of marrying a real prince, Prince Charles. Her later disappointment was perhaps, at least in part, due to the fact that in her youth, the saccharine novels she devoured created a fantasy world reality could simply never live up to. As Barbara Cartland put it, "The only books she ever read were mine and they weren't awfully good for her."[698]

Reading quality newspapers was also not her thing. At breakfast she read the emotionally charged *Daily Mail*, she was a "complete press addict" and devoured tabloid gossip about celebrities and royal families.[699] From her point of view, this was entirely rational. Her precise knowledge of these media helped her a lot in what she was to become a master of – self-marketing – which included a thorough knowledge of the press that was most relevant to her.

She was not only an avid consumer of tabloid news. To her, the journalists and paparazzi that had been stalking her everywhere since the beginning of her liaison with Prince Charles were not faceless snappers or hacks. "These were people whose stories she read. She even knew where they lived." Steve Wood of the *Daily Express* reports how he was once startled to see Diana standing outside his front door, checking out his address.[700]

Typically, journalists and photographers are interested in celebrities, but celebrities are far less interested in journalists and photographers. It was different with Diana. She knew precisely how to win over journalists and photographers. And she knew exactly which stories newspaper readers most wanted to read and which photos they most wanted to see. "She understood the popular press because she was their audience. She 'got' that audiences need to be fed with pictures and dreams, its requirement of novelty and surprise, its yearning to find a newcomer and crown her Queen. Forget *The Times* and *The Daily Telegraph*, the traditional house organs of the Establishment."[701]

According to her biographer, Diana was "the most artful practitioner" at playing the media game in the world. "She was way ahead of her contemporaries in foreseeing a world where celebrity was, so to speak, the coin of the realm ... An aristocrat, Diana knew that the aristocracy of birth was now irrelevant. All that counted now was the aristocracy of exposure."[702] The countless cameras that were trained on her exerted a fatal attraction. People who knew Diana well described her as having a "sixth sense" that told her when a camera was pointed in her direction, even if she couldn't see it for herself. The camera "had created the image that had given her so much power, and she was addicted to its magic, even when it hurt."[703]

One of the pack of photographers that followed Diana for years was convinced that her public image, including her famous shyness, was largely the result of careful and deliberate staging. In reality, the photographer confessed, the image of the "shy Di" was nothing more than a myth and only came about because she would lower her head, causing her hair to fall in front of her face. As a result, she was forced to look up from time to time simply to see where the photographers were.[704] Although otherwise not an analytical person, she developed analytical sharpness when it came to PR. Diana's sister had her own failed romance with Prince Charles and Diana thoroughly analyzed all of her sister's mistakes in this affair.[705]

She also avoided the clumsiness of favoring some journalists and neglecting others. "There was no indication of favoritism after she married Charles," said Ashley Walton, of the *Daily Express*. "We were all talked to and she would make a point of coming over and talking to us all."[706]

Diana had made it her business to get to know the editors and chairman of every important media outlet – just as, back when she was a young, unmarried woman, she had gotten to know the journalists who stalked her.[707] She invited key newspaper editors to a private lunch at Kensington Palace. "An encounter with the Princess on her own turf became a full-on multimedia experience combining all she had learned and wanted to project," explained her biographer. And the chief editor of a society magazine reported: "Everything went into the performance of Being Diana."[708]

She always used new methods to co-opt journalists and to cultivate special relationships to win the press over to her side. One of these methods consisted in entrusting a secret to someone she wanted to manipulate. It was "as if her fragile privacy was suddenly in his or her (usually his) hands."[709]

As reports of her difficult marriage became more widespread and more intense, Diana realized that she would have to change the way she worked to shape her public image. She knew she needed to get her side of the story out, but make it look as if any revelations came from sources other than herself. She settled on a book, which she could use to present her unhappy marriage in such a way that only her husband – Prince Charles – would be blamed and she would appear as a victim: as an unloved, sensitive and deceived woman who had longed for the prince's love, but got no more than his cold shoulder in return. Of course, she could not write the book herself. She found an author and gave him access to her friends, family and acquaintances. Despite the key role she played behind the scenes, Diana was never quoted in the book and publicly denied several times that she had ever cooperated with the author.[710] In reality, she had complete approval of the text, read every word of the book before its publication and even added her own handwritten revisions in the manuscript's margins. In early 1992, as the book's publication date was rapidly approaching, she wrote to a friend: "Obviously we are preparing for the volcano to erupt and I do feel better equipped for whatever comes our way."[711]

Her strategy quickly paid off. Excerpts from Andrew Morton's revelatory book *Diana: Her True Story*, which Diana herself had initiated, were published by *The Sunday Times* ahead of the book's official launch. "Diana Driven to Five Suicide Bids by 'Uncaring' Charles" was the banner headline across the top of page one. The article's subhead was "Marriage Collapse Led to Illness; Princess Says She Will Not Be Queen."[712] Diana had perfectly judged the public's subsequent reaction. "With the Morton revelations she had forged a visceral connection with millions. She had a fan base, a sisterhood."[713]

Whereas Diana acted like a media professional, her far more educated husband Prince Charles was entirely the opposite: a bumbling PR amateur. When he read the headlines, his response was emphatic: "I never want to see that paper in this house again! And as for the tabloids, I don't want to see any of them either. If anyone wants them, they will have to find them themselves – and that includes Her Royal Highness."[714] He simply refused to listen to the news or read the newspaper, explaining: "The last thing I want to do is get up in the morning and read what my bloody crazy wife has been doing."[715]

With the publication of the book, Diana had broken one of the royal family's strongest taboos. She had exposed the truth about her private relationships and the Windsors' internal affairs in public, something that would have been completely unthinkable in the past. However, she had managed to shape the narrative and it was her interpretation of her marriage to Charles that most people now accepted. Diana's skillful handling of the media and her professionalism in PR show that, although she was not very well educated by conventional standards and not particularly intelligent, she was one of the true geniuses in the art of self-marketing. "Charles," according to her biographer, "may have read more, but Diana was a swift, decisive executive in her own cause … She *was* a director in a sense, of her own *mise-en-scène*."[716]

At the age of 31, she was separated from her husband and set about "administering her celebrity like a global brand. Her life was now devoted to tending, promoting, and conserving the Diana franchise."[717] Diana's office at St. James's Palace increasingly came to resemble the reception hall of an advertising agency, with two huge frames filled with photo spreads from various magazines documenting her triumphs as a princess. She had a small, but astute team that developed professional PR strategies and thought about her commitments strategically.[718]

However, the successful Diana brand was stained when it became publicly known that she was literally terrorizing one of her lovers, a married man, by telephone. He was married to a wealthy woman from whom he did not want to separate under any circumstances, and Diana called him up to 20 times a day, even in the middle of the night. Once the press got hold of the story, their coverage was not entirely sympathetic. But Diana was always dreaming up new PR moves to put herself in the right light, which meant above all: portraying herself as a deceived victim, as a woman who only longed for the love she never got from her cold-hearted husband, who had been cheating on her from the very beginning with his ex-girlfriend Camilla Parker-Bowles.

Diana's greatest PR coup was a television interview with the journalist Martin Bashir. She had spent weeks practicing her lines and the interview was finally broadcast on November 14, 1995. On the night of the broadcast, the streets of London were deserted. Twenty-three million British viewers sat transfixed in front of their television sets[719] – and what they saw was a carefully crafted performance that hit all the right notes. Like a PR script, she had developed certain core messages that did not fail to have the desired effect:

- "I'd like to be a queen of people's hearts …"
- "There were three of us in the marriage." (A reference to Camilla Parker Bowles)
- "The Establishment that I married into – they have decided that I'm a nonstarter …"[720]
- (About the motives of her opponents): "I think it was out of fear, because here was a strong woman doing her bit, and where was she getting her strength from to continue?"[721]

She told her story in a way that every wronged woman could identify with. Asked about her own affair with James Hewitt, she avoided admitting to a sexual relationship, deftly brushed aside the question of a physical relationship and shifted to the emotional, saying, "Yes, I adored him. Yes, I was in love with him. But I was very let down."[722]

The public responded as she knew they would. She won their support by helping them to identify with her struggles and her complaints about the "Establishment" that had "decided" she was a failure. And although she was by no means a feminist, she tapped into the feminist zeitgeist by framing any criticism of her as resistance to an independent and strong woman "who was doing her bit" in her very own way.

Diana's core messages had their desired effect. On the Wednesday after the interview aired, a survey by the *Daily Mirror* showed 92 percent approval for Diana's television appearance. Even two weeks later, in a survey commissioned by *The Sunday Times*, 67 percent still said she had been right to give the interview, 70 percent were of the opinion that she should work as an international goodwill ambassador and only 25 percent thought it would be better if she played a less active role in public life.[723]

Expressing her desire to become a "Queen of People's Hearts," Diana had concisely and memorably formulated her key brand message – and had done so just as well as Steve Jobs did when he first marketed his iPhone.

So, how did Diana position herself? Of course, she could not just rely on her good looks. Diana – very astutely in this respect – recognized early on that it would have been completely impossible for her to try to shine in intellectual or political arenas. Why try to compete in domains where she could only lose and embarrass herself? Her positioning, her USP, was the "Queen of People's Hearts."

Psychologically, Diana was an extremely unstable woman with serious problems: she suffered from bulimia; after a fight with her husband, she cut her chest and thighs with a pocket knife; she seemed unable to develop a normal, harmonious or loving relationship with any of her partners, and was apparently completely unable to have a functioning relationship; normal friendships were also very difficult for her. The number of her outcast friends grew almost daily. A confidante reported: "There wasn't one friend that she hadn't fallen out with at one time or another."[724]

The paradox with Diana, writes her biographer, was, "that the woman who was so genuinely compassionate with strangers was capable of being cruelly dismissive of people closest to her."[725] She sought comfort and advice for her problems from obscure astrologers, parapsychologists, palm readers and graphologists. Diana was under the spell of these charlatans.[726]

But this was only one side of Diana. Like many people with psychological problems, she was extremely empathetic to the needs of others, especially those she did not know. Her biographer put it so aptly, "She plumbed the unhappiness of her own life and turned it into empathy."[727]

She probably suffered from what the psychoanalyst Wolfgang Schmidbauer described as the "helper syndrome" in his book, *Helpless Helpers*. The term refers to a pattern of mental problems that are often found among helping professions. As a consequence of their special personality, "helpers" try to compensate for their own feelings of inferiority by becoming fixated on their roles as helpers. In its most extreme form, their willingness to help can even lead to self-harm and neglect of family and other relationships, which can result in burnout or depression.

Diana, according to her biographer, "flowered in the presence of the disabled or sick." In a second, she was able to switch from the irritable and self-absorbed princess to a helper with a deep connection to people and a commitment to those in need.[728] When she left her own world to visit a hospital or a homeless shelter, it was "never royal condescension."[729] In the last interview before her death, which she gave to the newspaper *Le Monde*, she said "I'm much closer to the people at the bottom than the people at the top."[730]

She understandably had difficulties in dealing with intellectuals. But she knew how to turn her deficit, namely her lack of education and conventional intelligence, into an advantage. "The Princess's own intellectual insecurity was an unexpected asset. It made her head immediately for the underdog in any room – the aged, the shy, the very young."[731] Her mother once said of Diana: "She didn't speak to confident people half as easily as those who weren't ... She wasn't all that confident herself, she knew she had this gift with people and she used it wisely and generously."[732]

There are hundreds of accounts of Diana's magical charisma and her seemingly boundless empathy for the poor, weak and sick. One eyewitness recalled: "There was a radiance and a warmth about her as well as her beauty. One could sense her vulnerability. I noticed how she leaned over and listened so attentively to one of the caregivers, giving her full attention. A year later, the caregiver was still moved by it. She saw it as a key experience in her life. It was as if everyone there that morning had been touched by light."[733]

Another observer said that Diana had a special ability to create "pools of intimacy" with young offenders or disabled children. Even in the presence of television cameras, her listening gaze held the parent or the child she was talking to in a protective private circle.[734]

Again and again, Diana used her special kind of empathy to win over skeptical members of the press. One *Sunday Times* war reporter noticed how close Diana came to landmine victims. She was impressed that Diana never turned her head away from injuries so horrific that she herself could not look, even though she had been reporting from the Third World for years. "She had something I'd only ever seen before from Nelson Mandela," wrote the reporter, "a kind of aura that made people want to be with her and a completely natural, straight-from-the-heart sense of how to bring hope to those who seemed to have little to live for."[735]

One of Diana's friends described a conversation Diana had with a woman who had suffered countless miscarriages and was so desperate that she burst into tears. "All her sadness just come pouring out, and Diana suddenly switched from being that person who was worried about her own future to being a person who was incredibly compassionate. She was able to home in on them and get to the core of them in a way which was extraordinary."[736] An Australian journalist reported on one of Diana's encounters with children: "She would get down, bend down and talk to small children. She was just so different, so much closer to the people. It was brilliant for us – it provided good stories every single day."[737]

Every day a "good story" – that was the secret of Diana's success: she combined her special gift of empathy with her unique talent for PR. She was virtually addicted to articles about herself. After a tour of Australia and New Zealand, she began to skim through the newspapers every morning for pictures of herself, starting with the tabloids, before moving on to the broadsheets.[738] "She was a complete press addict," claimed one journalist from the *Daily Express*. "She would read everything about herself right from the beginning and knew exactly who had written what. We know that because she would remark on a particular story to us. When she was living at Highgrove she would take some money and go into Tetbury where she would buy armfuls of newspapers and magazines. We used to doorstep the newsagents. If her picture was on the cover, she would buy the magazine."[739]

On the one hand she complained about the paparazzi who surrounded her, on the other hand she was distressed when the cameras were not trained on her. "Whenever she wasn't out being the People's Princess, she was inside her cage, wondering what to do with all that energy and charisma, which could find outlet only in the adulation of others."[740]

It is difficult for an outside observer to distinguish between what was authentic and natural in Diana's life and what was staged – she probably didn't always know herself. In the foreword to the German edition of Tina Brown's biography, the journalist Patricia Dreyer observed: "Initially, her inimitable doe-eyed expression was due to her shyness, which she has long since overcome. Then it owed everything to her camera-conscious calculation. Her commitment to those society has left behind – people suffering with AIDS, the homeless – originally flowed from her genuine helper ethos. But what has always been a matter of the heart can also become a weapon: Diana chose to be the patron of projects that other royals avoided."[741] This allowed her to seem more human and progressive. And it enabled her to rekindle many people's affections for the British monarchy, which had, until Diana, been regarded as traditionalist, elitist and remote.

As with many others who become incredibly famous, she developed a tendency toward megalomania, which she used to compensate for her inferiority complex. Once, over a meal, she casually told those around the table that she could resolve the "troubles" in Northern Ireland, where a civil war that had cost thousands of lives had been raging since the late 1960s. "I'm very good at sorting people's heads out," was how she justified her optimism that she could resolve the conflict.[742]

Diana knew how to turn her inferiority complexes and psychological weaknesses into highly effective assets. Her lack of education helped her develop a close rapport with the general public; she turned her psychological conditions into a helper syndrome; and her own deep-seated vulnerability formed the basis for her empathy – allowing her to transform herself into the Queen of People's Hearts.

Tools Diana used to build her brand:

1. She did not engage in competition in areas where she could only lose (intellectual issues or issues where knowledge and education were important). She turned her weakness – vulnerability and her helper syndrome – into a strength.

2. From the very beginning, she was very active in press relations and cultivated personal relationships with editors and photographers. She was interested in journalists as people.

3. She used all the tools of PR – most notably an expository book she commissioned and a major television interview. She beat Charles, who had gone from being the prince of her dreams to her adversary, with her side of the story, thus setting the framework for interpretation.

4. She repeatedly broke taboos by speaking openly about difficulties and problems in her marriage and in her relationship with the royal family.

5. She professionally devised memorable and effective core messages for her PR, e.g.: "I'd like to be a queen of people's hearts."

6. Despite her elevated social status, she was very close to the people and not arrogant. She made her empathy for the weak her USP.

7. She provided the media and the public with a victim framing for the interpretation of her failed marriage: "There were three of us in the marriage"; "The Establishment that I married into – they have decided that I'm a nonstarter."

CHAPTER TWELVE

KIM KARDASHIAN WEST: FAMOUS FOR BEING FAMOUS

(WFPA / Alamy Stock Photo)

Kim Kardashian West has 236 million followers on Instagram, even more than Lionel Messi (233 million), the record winner of the FIFA World Player of the Year Award with six titles since 2009. On Twitter, Kim has 69 million followers, almost as many as former American President Donald Trump had before he was banned (well over 70 million)[743] and more than CNN's breaking news feed (58 million). So, what does it take to achieve a degree of popularity on social media comparable to that of the most powerful politician and the best soccer player in the world? Kim is a member of the Kardashian-Jenner family, who have established themselves as one of the richest celebrity families in the U.S. Her half-sister Kylie Jenner has been named the youngest self-made billionaire in history by *Forbes*.[744]

Famous people often claim that as children they made it clear that they wanted to become famous later in life, but this is rarely verifiable. In Kim's case, there is actually a video that shows her as a 13-year-old who states "Is anyone getting a tape of this? I hope you do, because when you see me when I'm famous and old, you're gonna remember me as this beautiful little girl."[745] Many young people dream of becoming famous. But how did Kim manage to turn this dream into a reality?

Her father, Robert Kardashian, gained some notoriety as the close friend and lawyer of the football player O.J. Simpson, whom he defended in one of the most high-profile murder trials in the United States. If Kim, born in 1980, was casually mentioned in the early 2000s, it was at best as the daughter of O.J. Simpson's lawyer.[746]

From the beginning, one of Kim's strategies for success was that she sought the company of people who were much more famous than she was herself. She started with a business idea that would connect her with celebrities: Kim organized their overflowing wardrobes and auctioned off clothes they no longer needed on eBay. She won prominent clients such as Cindy Crawford and Serena Williams[747] and became known as the "Queen of the Closet Scene,"[748] a reference to the dramatic "closet scene" in Shakespeare's Hamlet, where a person hides in the prince's mother's dressing room. One of Kim's prominent clients was the hotel heiress Paris Hilton, who was only a few months younger and was soon to become one of Kim's major role models.

Paris Hilton and her sister signed a contract with Fox television network in 2003 to star in the new reality show, *The Simple Life*, which would be broadcast from December 2003. A few weeks earlier, the Page Six column of the tabloid newspaper *New York Post*, known for its celebrity gossip, was the first to report that there was a sex tape with Paris Hilton. The material showing the 23-year-old and her boyfriend, Rick Salomon, having sex and oral sex with each other was recorded in May 2001. Hilton's boyfriend, a professional poker player and former drug dealer, had often videoed himself having sex with his girlfriends. These home movies were obviously not shot for publication, but for private use. Nevertheless, Salomon offered the video on his personal website for $50 a copy and then negotiated a distribution agreement with the adult film company Red Light District Video. It is said that Paris Hilton agreed to release the video in exchange for a payment of $400,000 and a share in profits. The video helped to popularize Hilton's reality show, *The Simple Life*, which was launched shortly thereafter.

Kim Kardashian admired Hilton as a role model and the PR surrounding the sex tape that helped to get the reality show noticed was an important lesson in media exposure. Kim was completely unknown at the time, but she now frequently appeared in photos as one of Paris Hilton's friends as they spent nights together prowling the hip clubs of Los Angeles. Elliot Mintz, who worked for Hilton as a PR consultant (and had represented such prominent musicians as John Lennon, Yoko Ono and Bob Dylan in the past), observed that Kim was very different from other young women in the club scene: she was always gracious and extremely polite, she was not a drinker or substance abuser, and she was always very punctual.[749] And she never made the mistake of trying to steal the show from Paris. Kim learned eagerly from Paris, and her biographer Sean Smith observed, "If you look at many of the things she later attempted, they were tried first by Paris."[750] It later became clear, Smith said, "how many aspects of the Kim Kardashian story would mirror the celebrity branding of Paris Hilton, whether consciously or unconsciously."[751] Kim Kardashian's celebrity career also began with a sex tape and a subsequent reality show. Kim's boyfriend at the time, rapper Ray J, had also recorded a video in October 2003 of them having sex. Although they claimed that the video was never meant for others to see, doubts are justified. For example, one scene shows Kim walking from the bathroom into the bedroom, the camera follows her as she turns and says into the camera: "To all of you out there who think my boobs are fake, they're real." A statement that's obviously not addressed only to Ray J.[752]

In the winter of 2006, rumors about the existence of the sex tape started to circulate, which Kim initially denied. How the footage came into the possession of Vivid Entertainment, one of the leading distributors of pornography in the United States, remains hotly disputed to this day. At the time the tape became public, Kim's mother, Kris Jenner, had negotiated a contract with the TV station E! for a reality show about the life of the Kardashian family. In his biography *The Kardashians*, Jerry Oppenheimer quotes an insider who claims that, "Kris [Kim's mother] saw the value in that tape, knew how a sex tape had made Paris Hilton a sensation, and figured it could do the same for Kim. Either directly or indirectly, that tape got to the folks of Vivid. Kris knew what she was doing, and Kim went along for the ride. It was all about money and fame."[753] In contrast, Kim's biographer Sean Smith reports that Kim's mother was horrified when she learned of the existence of the home-made sex tape.[754]

Kim sued Vivid Entertainment to try and prevent the release of the video, which they wanted to release as *Kim Kardashian, Superstar*. "Ironically, the media interest in the sex tape created by Kim's legal action was just the sort of publicity that would guarantee its success."[755] Without the lawsuit, the video would certainly not have been such a success. After lengthy negotiations, Vivid, Kim and her ex-boyfriend Ray J agreed a deal that allegedly awarded her $5 million for withdrawing her lawsuit, another several hundred thousand dollars and, most importantly, a share of the royalties from the tape. The video became one of the most successful sex tapes of all time[756] and Kim Kardashian became not only a millionaire in her own right,[757] but – just like Paris Hilton – Kim used the scandalous video as the perfect PR platform to launch her new reality show, *Keeping Up with the Kardashians*. The show was first broadcast on the E! channel on October 14, 2007. As of today, there have been a total of 280 episodes spread across 20 seasons.[758] In the first four weeks alone, the show drew more than 13 million viewers. The sex tape wasn't the only PR publicity stunt that boosted Kim's profile: In December 2007, she appeared on the cover of *Playboy* and the shoot for the men's magazine was documented in an episode of the reality show.[759]

The timing could not have been better as it coincided perfectly with the start of the series. First there were the rumors of a sex tape, then Kim's lawsuit to block its distribution, which is what really sparked public attention, followed by the release of *Kim Kardashian, Superstar* and finally the start of the reality series and the cover of *Playboy*. But how was Kim's plan to become famous supposed to proceed? After the start of the series she swore to herself: "I promised myself that this year I would do things that are kind of outside my comfort zone."[760]

At first, all she knew was *that* she wanted to become incredibly famous, but she did not know *how*. It would have been obvious for a young, attractive woman to strive for a career as a film actress or as a singer, and Kim tried both – but without success. Ironically, her first film, *Disaster Movie*, was a disaster, and came 14th in an *Empire* online poll of the 50 worst movies of all time.[761] *The Observer* wrote, "It would be the Worst Movie Ever Made were it actually a movie at all."[762] Kim was even nominated for the Golden Raspberry Award for Worst Supporting Actress in 2008.[763]

After her unsuccessful film debut, she tried to become famous as a dancer – another well-trodden path for young, wannabe starlets. She took part in the ABC show, *Dancing With the Stars*, but dropped out after only one week.[764] Despite the setback, Kim did not give up and shifted her focus to being a singer. Her single, "Jam (Turn it Up)," also flopped with only 14,000 downloads in its first week on iTunes.[765] Upon reflection, she admitted, "What gave me the right to think I could be a singer? Like, I don't have a good voice."[766]

But Kim did not give up. The most important goal in her life was to become famous and she would do anything to achieve it. The music producer Damon Thomas, Kim's husband for three years, highlighted the negative side of her ambitions: "Kim is obsessed with fame. She can't write or sing or dance, so she does harmful things in order to validate herself in the media. That's a fame-whore to me."[767]

What set Kim apart was her incredible work ethic, determination and tolerance for frustration. She was known as a workaholic and her older sister Kourtney once observed, "She's dating her work."[768] Despite all the failed attempts to make it as an actress, dancer and singer, she held on to her great dream of fame. "You have to stay committed," she explained. "Some people start and stop, or get a bit lazy. Every year my mom and I write out a goal sheet"[769] – a technique she shares with many very successful people. As her biographer Smith writes, "It was as if Kim stood in front of a mirror and decided how best utilize every bit of herself from top to bottom and head to toe. She would take every opportunity that came her way and make sure she was personally involved and not just a celebrity robot."[770]

Kim's success was and is based on her mastery of social media, whose potential she recognized earlier than many others and which she has exploited more skillfully than many millions of young women who want to become rich and famous as "influencers." By the beginning of 2010, she already had more than 2.7 million followers and was rumored to have been paid $10,000 for recommending a particular salad on Twitter: "I'm on my way to Carl's Jr. for lunch now … Have you tried them yet?"[771]

She was the face of very successful social media campaigns for CKE restaurants and other brands and finally launched her own perfume brand in February 2010.[772] The reality show, *Keeping Up with the Kardashians*, made her more and more famous and at the end of 2010, she topped the list of highest-earning reality TV stars with an estimated $6 million. In the same year, there were more online searches for Kim than for U.S. President Barack Obama or superstar Justin Bieber.[773] She was paid up to $100,000 just for turning up at a club.[774] And by July 2010, a statue of Kim was on display in Madame Tussauds wax museum in New York City.[775]

If at first Kim thought she needed to be exceptional – either as an actress, singer or dancer – she soon realized that social media would allow her to become famous for being famous, as the pejorative term would have it. All it takes is the right launch – in Kim's case the sex tape and the reality series – followed by relentless work to build the brand. "The branding philosophy of the Kardashians was simple: first, extend your brand as far as you can and always react to situations – if you put on weight, land a deal to promote diet supplement pills; secondly, be as visible and share as much as possible – the public are as interested in the bad times as the good; thirdly, use Facebook, Twitter, Instagram and any other online method you can think of to connect with the public."[776]

She mainly posts photos, and like most self-marketers, she has made a certain external feature her USP. Just as Schwarzenegger had his biceps, Karl Lagerfeld had his braid, sunglasses and stand-up collar, Donald Trump has his hair and Albert Einstein his nutty professor look, Kim Kardashian has her bottom. When she won the Entrepreneur of the Year award at the Glamour Women of the Year Awards in London in June 2011, interest in her buttocks was so great that they were actually X-rayed to determine whether they were real or contained implants.[777] In an episode of *Keeping Up with the Kardashians*, she shows how she had her backside X-rayed by the doctor and then her nurses post the X-ray.[778] It proved her booty was real – and Kim let the whole world know.

In subsequent years, however, there were regular debates on the internet and in the media as to whether her bottom was genuine or the product of cosmetic surgery. Kim succeeded time and again in attracting attention with spectacular shots that focus on her backside. Two years later, the reputable *Daily Telegraph* reported on one particular image that attracted an enormous amount of attention: "In September 2014 niche title *Paper Magazine* created one of the biggest cultural events of the year, and perhaps the decade, when they set out to 'Break The Internet' with the help of a naked Kim Kardashian. The image of Kim Kardashian balancing a champagne glass on her perfectly-sculpted derriere alongside the hashtag #BreakTheInternet sent a sharing shockwave through the web. The site received over 50 million hits in one day, equating to 1 per cent of all internet traffic that day in the US."[779]

Mickey Boardman, editor of *Paper*, remarked about the magazine's cover: "At the time, we thought it would be an amazing cover. We had no idea what a humongous cultural phenomenon it would be. There are a lot of celebrities who don't want to do anything too risky, but we had a feeling Kim wanted to do something wild, something iconic, and that's exactly what happened."[780] Kim was never afraid to polarize, a fact that also helped her to build her brand. "People always have some kind of reaction to her. Either they *love* Kim or they think she's a symbol of *everything* that's wrong with society. There are very few people who elicit that strong of a reaction."[781]

One of the keys to Kim's and the Kardashians' success was that their brand was never just about one person, but a whole family. The value of the overall Kardashian brand has always increased whenever one of the many family members was in the news. Mother Kris, who calls herself "Momager," played a central role in this success. The Kardashians, as Erin Klazas puts it in an analysis of the phenomenon, are a family that stands for a special form of individualism: "It is a kind of *collective* individualism. Through strong bonds with each other, the sisters promote one brand set out for empowerment, and are the product of collective self-entrepreneurship."[782]

Sometimes it was not clear what was reality and what was merely a stunt for her reality show. One example of this is Kim's marriage to basketball star Kris Humphries, who proposed to her in May with a $2-million ring. A two-part episode of the wedding was watched by 4.4 million and 4 million viewers respectively. But only 72 days after the marriage, Kim filed for divorce.[783]

From the beginning, she had chosen her friends, lovers and husbands according to their "celebrity factor." She worked her way up the celebrity ladder from bottom to top and each new partner was a little more famous than the previous one. In April 2012, Kim officially announced her relationship with Kanye West,[784] in May 2014 they married. Kanye West was and is one of the most prominent hip hop and pop musicians in the world. In recognition of his impact on popular culture, *Time* magazine featured West in its lists of the 100 most influential people in the world for the first time in 2005 and again in 2015. Unlike many other rappers, he had not grown up on the street, never sold drugs or hustled. He had studied English literature at Chicago State, but then dropped out.[785] The marriage gave Kim another huge publicity boost. Both were in the headlines constantly. In August 2014, the media reported that they had bought a $20 million estate and, to guarantee their privacy, the house next door for $2.9 million.[786]

The name Kim Kardashian increasingly became synonymous with "becoming famous," which also happens to be the theme of a video game, *Kim Kardashian: Hollywood*, which she released in July 2014. In the same way that Monopoly is about getting rich, the goal in Kim's game is to become famous. Each player must try to move up from an "E-list" to an "A-list" celebrity, just as Kim did in real life.

It is said that Kim was instrumental in the game's 18-month development process. Players can gain more fans in the game by taking on modeling or acting jobs, appearing in hip clubs or dating celebrities.[787] According to an analysis of the game: "Selling the self via personal branding is the route to celebrity success … The results across these activities are also identical – the ever-present and watching media will report positively or negatively on your professional activity… Effective self-representation and the ability to circulate the representation across the necessary media platforms become the fundamental element of fame …"[788] Just a few months after *Kim Kardashian: Hollywood* was released, it had nearly 23 million players. According to *Forbes*, Kim's income rose from $28 million to $53 million between 2014 and 2015. The success of her game played a major role in boosting her wealth.[789]

The TV series, her video game, and all of Kim's and the Kardashian family's other activities were mutually reinforcing, but the core was always TV. In February 2015, the Kardashians signed a $100 million contract for the next four years of the series, which has since been broadcast in 160 countries.[790] In 2018, *Forbes* estimated Kim's personal fortune at $350 million,[791] with her company, KKR Beauty, being the main contributor to her wealth, and in 2021 she became a billionaire. According to *The*

New York Times, the strength of her brand was confirmed when KKR Beauty was founded: "In the first five minutes of Kim introducing her KKW Beauty line in 2017, she sold an estimated $14.4 million worth of product (or about 300,000 items)."[792]

As early as 1968 the artist Andy Warhol predicted: "In the future, everyone will be world-famous for 15 minutes." In pre-capitalist times, fame was a privilege reserved for nobles, members of royal families. Under capitalism, fame was democratized – the promise was now that anyone, regardless of birth, gender or origin, could become famous for their achievements, skill or talent, for example as an actor or pop star. Over the years, it has become more and more apparent that achievement alone is no guarantee for fame – it needs to be combined with the art of self-marketing, which involves showcasing achievements in the right light and letting everyone know about them. This art of self-marketing, as Kim's example shows particularly clearly, has decoupled itself from actual achievement in the age of the internet. To be more precise: the real achievement today is the art of self-marketing.

Brandon Boileau sums this up in an essay on Kim's success: "Hollywood celebrities used to be held in high esteem as heroes of the normalization and excessive presence of the entertainment industry in all areas of life. It is increasingly possible today to enter the celebrity realm via unconditional points of entry with the help of the internet and the large reach of the entertainment industry."[793] Kim's success proves to her fans that you don't have to first make it as a singer, actress or dancer to become famous – there is a far shorter path to fame. Potentially anyone can become famous, they just have to want it, dedicate their life to it and understand and master the mechanisms of self-marketing.

The major attraction of Kim and other social media stars (influencers, etc.) is that every young woman can identify with them, because their celebrity would seem to confirm that fame awaits anyone who wants it enough and is willing to pay the price. For critics, this fame appears to be an "undeserved" achievement, but this is based on a misunderstanding. According to her biographer Sean Smith, Kim is "a consummate professional in all she does. She continues to be derided as devoid of talent, as if winning a television dance contest would in some way legitimize her success, huge wealth, lovely home and a family that loves her. If what she did were easy and everyone could do it, there would be a million Kim Kardashians out there, but there aren't. There is only one."[794]

When biographer Jerry Oppenheimer critically notes that the Kardashians have "little or no discernable talent besides self-promotion,"[795] it sounds as if the art of self-marketing is not a "real" talent and that the fame it creates is somehow undeserved. This was also the opinion of the TV presenter Barbara Walters, who didn't mince her words when she reproached Kim, "You don't really act; you don't sing; you don't dance,... You don't have any – forgive me – any talent!"[796] But this is wrong. For many of the famous people portrayed in this book, the art of self-marketing played at least as important a role as their achievements in their actual professions – as scientists or athletes, for example. Self-marketing is a *sui generis* art, and this is particularly evident in a family such as the Kardashians, because it is mainly the mastery of the principles of marketing and PR that has made them so successful.

Tools Kim Kardashian West used to build her brand:

1. From the very beginning, Kim sought the company of celebrities such as Paris Hilton in order to raise her own profile – she studied their success closely and learned what it takes to attract attention.

2. She gives millions of women who post on social media the hope that they, too, could become rich and famous – without mastering anything other than the art of self-marketing. "The Kardashians have become models for young women seeking success through self-branding."[797]

3. Perseverance plus a willingness to experiment is one of Kim's formulas for success: She first tried to become famous in the traditional way, but her efforts as an actress, dancer and singer all failed. She didn't give up and found her own way to fame via social media and a reality show.

4. Attracting attention without worrying about social norms was another recipe for her success. Her career began with a scandal over a sex tape.

5. Focus, extreme discipline and work ethic are not typical characteristics for young women in the world of fashion, but in Kim's view they are decisive factors for success: "When I was in my early twenties, a lot of young people were just concerned with going out and partying and drinking. I do believe that a lot of my success is due to the fact that I've always been in control of my lifestyle. I've always been really committed to something. I definitely think that it can be discouraging. It can be exhausting. But you really do have to put the time in and put the work in. And really just stay focused."[798]

6. She turned her curvaceous derrière into a trademark and USP: Just as Schwarzenegger had his biceps, Karl Lagerfeld had his braid, sunglasses and stand-up collar, Donald Trump has his hair and Albert Einstein his nutty professor look, Kim Kardashian has her bottom, which has been the focus of thousands of photos and videos.

ABOUT THE AUTHOR

Rainer Zitelmann was born in Frankfurt am Main, Germany in 1957. He studied history and political science from 1978 to 1983 and graduated with distinction. In 1986, he was awarded the title Dr. phil for his thesis *Hitler: The Policies of Seduction* under the mentorship of Professor Freiherr von Aretin. The study received the highest possible grade, summa cum laude, and generated worldwide attention and recognition.

He then went on to lecture history at the Free University of Berlin from 1987 to 1992, before becoming editor-in-chief at one of the leading and most prestigious publishing houses in Germany, Ullstein-Propyläen. He followed this by taking up the role of section editor at the major German daily newspaper *Die Welt*, a position he held until 2000, when he embarked on a career as an entrepreneur. He set up the public relations consultancy Dr. ZitelmannPB. GmbH, which he quickly established as by far the leading PR consultancy for the German real estate industry. He sold the business in 2016. Zitelmann built his wealth through his entrepreneurial activities and as a successful real estate investor.

In 2016, Zitelmann was awarded his second doctorate, this time in sociology, with his thesis on the psychology of the super-rich under the mentorship of Professor Wolfgang Lauterbach at the University of Potsdam. The study has been published in the United States, the UK, China and South Korea as *The Wealth Elite*.

Zitelmann has written a total of 25 books, which have enjoyed substantial success in a range of languages around the world. For example, his book *Dare to be Different and Grow Rich* has been published in 12 different languages alone. He is a popular guest speaker at events in Asia, the United States and across Europe. Over the last few years, he has written articles and given interviews to many of the world's leading media outlets, including *Le Monde*, *Corriere de la Serra*, *Frankfurter Allgemeine Zeitung*, *Die Welt*, *Neue Zürcher Zeitung*, *The Daily Telegraph*, *The Times* and numerous media in China and South Korea. More information on the life and career or Rainer Zitelmann is available at: www.rainer-zitelmann.com.

REFERENCES

Introduction

[1] Hawking, *Brief Answers*, 19.

[2] Levy, 152.

[3] Eig, 301.

[4] Schwarzenegger, 606.

[5] https://www.billboard.com/charts/greatest-hot-100-artists

[6] http://content.time.com/time/specials/packages/article/0,28804,2029774_2029776_2031853,00.html

[7] Camille Barbone quoted in O'Brien, 45–46.

[8] O'Brien, 213.

[9] As of July 31, 2021

[10] https://www.denverpost.com/2011/12/15/people-you-dont-have-talent-barbara-walters-tells-kardashians/

[11] Charlie Chaplin, quoted in Isaacson, *Einstein*, 374.

[12] Einstein, quoted in Illy, 319.

[13] Lagerfeld, quoted in Sahner, 228.

[14] D'Antonio, 442.

[15] Neffe, 362.

[16] Neffe, 293.

[17] Neffe, 293.

[18] Neffe, 373.

[19] Spohn, 29.

[20] Spohn, 45.

[21] Smith, 273.

[22] https://www.telegraph.co.uk/fashion/people/the-man-behind-kim-kardashians-paper-magazine-cover-on-how-to-br/

[23] Hawking, *My Brief History*, 122.

[24] Hawking, *My Brief History*, 99.

[25] Hawking, *My Brief History*, 90.

[26] D'Antonio, 427.

[27] Eig, 240–241.

[28] Neffe, 26.

[29] Jobs, quoted in Isaacson, *Jobs*, 296.

[30] Madonna, quoted in O'Brien, x.

[31] Taraborrelli, 97.

[32] O'Brien, 134.

[33] O'Brien, 151.

[34] O'Brien, S. 236.

[35] *The Observer*, quoted in O'Brien, 171.

[36] Taraborrelli, 237.

[37] O'Brien, 193.

[38] Taraborrelli, 240.

[39] Kelley, 97.

[40] Kelley, 11–13.

[41] Kelley, 7.

[42] Kelley, 6.

[43] Winfrey, quoted in Kelley, 239.

[44] Kelley, 239.

[45] Winfrey, quoted in Kelley, 260.

[46] Eig, 309.

[47] Eig, 328.

[48] Ali, quoted in Eig, 374.

[49] Eig, 503.

[50] Eig, 530.

[51] Indiana, 84.

[52] Hawking, *Brief Answers*, 141.

[53] Hawking, *My Brief History*, 98.

[54] Ali, quoted in Hauser, 41.

[55] Schwarzenegger, 68.

[56] Schwarzenegger, 389.

[57] Schwarzenegger, 388.

[58] Brown, 466.

[59] Diana, quoted in Brown, 473.

[60] Diana, quoted in Brown, 468.

[61] Diana, quoted in Brown, 473.

[62] Schwarzenegger, quoted in Andrews, 61.

[63] Schwarzenegger, quoted in Andrews, 74.

[64] This and other examples in Goldsmith, xi–xii.

[65] Warhol, quoted in Goldsmith, xiii.

[66] Warhol, quoted in Goldsmith, xiv.
[67] Einstein, quoted in Calaprice, 275.
[68] Trump, quoted in Kranish/Fisher, 104.
[69] Eig, 39.
[70] Eig, 84–85.
[71] Ali, quoted in Hauser, 54–55.
[72] Trump on Twitter, May 9, 2013.
[73] Winfrey, quoted in Kelley, 117.
[74] Lagerfeld, quoted in Sahner, 11.
[75] Hertzfeld, quoted in Isaacson, *Jobs*, 109.
[76] Erica Bell recalls a conversation with Madonna, quoted in Taraborrelli, 79.
[77] Madonna, quoted in Taraborrelli, 9.
[78] Madonna, quoted in Taraborrelli, 125.
[79] Indiana, xii.
[80] Indiana, 14.
[81] Spohn, 29.
[82] Spohn, 57–58.
[83] Koestenbaum, 155.
[84] Kranish/Fisher, 99.
[85] Kelley, 189.
[86] Lagerfeld, quoted in Sahner, 232.
[87] Lagerfeld, quoted in Sahner, 312.
[88] Becker et al., *Der Spiegel*, 2019, No. 9, February 23, 2019.

Chapter 1

[89] Neffe, 9.
[90] Neffe, 9.
[91] Neffe, 261.
[92] Charlie Chaplin, quoted in Neffe, 366.
[93] Einstein, quoted in Calaprice, 14.
[94] Einstein, quoted in Illy, 319.
[95] Isaacson, *Einstein*, 266.
[96] Isaacson, *Einstein*, 267.
[97] Neffe, 350.
[98] Verse from Einstein, quoted in Neffe, 166.
[99] Neffe, 11.
[100] Neffe, 17–18.
[101] Neffe, 399–400.
[102] Isaacson, *Einstein*, 5.

[103] Neffe, 362.
[104] Neffe, 293.
[105] Neffe, 293.
[106] Neffe, 373.
[107] Neffe, 366.
[108] Neffe, 271.
[109] Neffe, 271.
[110] Ambassador Solf, quoted in Neffe, 275.
[111] Ambassador Solf, quoted in Neffe, 275.
[112] *Berliner Tageblatt*, quoted in Neffe, 273.
[113] Neffe, 361.
[114] Neffe, 359.
[115] Einstein, quoted in Neffe, 361.
[116] Einstein, quoted in Neffe, 364.
[117] Einstein, quoted in Neffe, 16.
[118] Quoted in Neffe, 374.
[119] *The New York Times*, quoted in Isaacson, *Einstein*, 266.
[120] Isaacson, *Einstein*, 266.
[121] Isaacson, *Einstein*, 268.
[122] C.P. Snow quoted in Isaacson, *Einstein*, 268–269.
[123] Freeman Dyson, quoted in Isaacson, *Einstein*, 269.
[124] Isaacson, *Einstein*, 270.
[125] Isaacson, *Einstein*, 270–271.
[126] Isaacson, *Einstein*, 273.
[127] Abraham Flexner quoted in Isaacson, *Einstein*, 429.
[128] Abraham Flexner quoted in Isaacson, *Einstein*, 430.
[129] Isaacson, *Einstein*, 431.
[130] Neffe, 26.
[131] Einstein, *Einstein on Peace*, quoted in Calaprice, 303.
[132] Einstein, quoted in Calaprice, 249.
[133] Einstein, quoted in Calaprice, 116.
[134] Einstein, quoted in Calaprice, 292.
[135] Einstein, quoted in Calaprice, 299.
[136] Einstein quoted in Calaprice, 275.
[137] Gustav Bucky quoted in Neffe, 29.
[138] Neffe, 116.
[139] Neffe, 116–117.
[140] Neffe, 152.
[141] Quoted in Neffe, 27.
[142] Einstein in a letter to Max Born, quoted in Calaprice, 8.

Chapter 2

[143] Skiena/Ward, 293.

[144] Indiana, 84.

[145] Spohn, 82.

[146] Spohn, 127.

[147] John Perrault, quoted in Bockris, 321.

[148] Warhol, quoted in Goldsmith, 196.

[149] Spohn, 70.

[150] Spohn, 126.

[151] Indiana, xv.

[152] Indiana, 65.

[153] Indiana, 111.

[154] Indiana, 112.

[155] Koestenbaum, 42.

[156] Warhol, quoted in Warhol/Hackett, 20.

[157] Indiana, 117.

[158] Indiana, 110.

[159] Indiana, 17.

[160] Valerie Solanas, quoted in Frank, 210.

[161] Warhol, quoted in Bockris, 311.

[162] Warhol, quoted in Bockris, 321.

[163] Spohn, 19.

[164] Spohn, 29.

[165] Spohn, 45.

[166] Warhol, quoted in Bockris, 347.

[167] Friends of Warhol, including Elaine Baumann, quoted in Bockris, 86.

[168] Vito Giallo, quoted in Bockris, 113.

[169] Koestenbaum, 5.

[170] Indiana, 141.

[171] Indiana, xiv.

[172] Indiana, 66.

[173] Indiana, 91.

[174] Indiana, 151.

[175] This and other examples in Goldsmith, xi–xii.

[176] Warhol, quoted in Goldsmith, xiii.

[177] Warhol, quoted in Goldsmith, xiv.

[178] Warhol quoted in: Goldsmith, xv.

[179] Goldsmith, xvi.

[180] Indiana, 125.

[181] Indiana, 68.

[182] Indiana, xii.

[183] Indiana, 14.

[184] Spohn, 29.

[185] Spohn, 57–58.

[186] Koestenbaum, 155.

[187] Koestenbaum, 147.

[188] Indiana, 131.

[189] Indiana, 150.

Chapter 3

[190] Lagerfeld, quoted in Sahner, 224.

[191] Sahner, 16.

[192] Sahner, 10.

[193] Lagerfeld, quoted in Sahner, 324.

[194] Lagerfeld, quoted in Sahner, 11.

[195] Lagerfeld, quoted in Sahner, 490.

[196] Lagerfeld, quoted in Sahner, 312.

[197] Lagerfeld, quoted in Sahner, 84.

[198] Lagerfeld, quoted in Sahner, 101.

[199] Lagerfeld, quoted in Sahner, 40.

[200] Lagerfeld, quoted in Sahner, 466.

[201] Lagerfeld, quoted in Sahner, 83.

[202] Lagerfeld, quoted in Sahner, 68.

[203] Lagerfeld, quoted in Sahner, 78.

[204] Lagerfeld, quoted in Sahner, 170.

[205] Sahner, 311.

[206] Maillard, 198.

[207] Maillard, 199.

[208] Sahner, 332.

[209] Lagerfeld, quoted in Sahner, 228.

[210] Sahner, 458.

[211] Lagerfeld, quoted in Sahner, 207.

[212] Lagerfeld, quoted in Sahner, 232.

[213] Lagerfeld, quoted in Sahner, 151.

[214] Sahner, 181.

[215] Lagerfeld, quoted in Sahner, 26.

[216] Sahner, 26.

[217] Wolfgang Joop, quoted in Sahner, 183–184.

[218] Lagerfeld, quoted in Sahner, 308.

[219] Lagerfeld, quoted in Sahner, 315.

[220] Sahner, 362.

[221] Lagerfeld, quoted in Sahner, 121.

[222] Lagerfeld, quoted in Sahner, 361.

[223] Lagerfeld, quoted in Sahner, 361.

[224] Lagerfeld, quoted in Sahner, 19–20.

[225] Maillard, 206.

[226] Lagerfeld, quoted in Sahner, 83.

[227] Lagerfeld, quoted in Sahner, 282.

[228] Lagerfeld, quoted in Sahner, 145.

[229] Becker et al., *Der Spiegel,* 2019, No. 9, February 23, 2019.

[230] Maillard, 197–198.

[231] Lagerfeld, quoted in Sahner, 397.

[232] Lagerfeld, quoted in Sahner, 464.

[233] Lagerfeld, quoted in Sahner, 472.

[234] Lagerfeld, quoted in Sahner, 406.

[235] Lagerfeld, quoted in Sahner, 463.

Chapter 4

[236] Hawking, *My Brief History*, 46.

[237] Levy, 25.

[238] Levy, 25.

[239] Hawking, *My Brief History*, 48.

[240] Hawking, *My Brief History*, 49.

[241] Hawking, *My Brief History*, 122.

[242] Hawking, *My Brief History*, 123.

[243] White/Gribbin, 164–165.

[244] Hawking, *Brief Answers*, 15

[245] Hawking, *Brief Answers*, 19.

[246] Levy, 152.

[247] Levy, 134.

[248] Hawking, *My Brief History*, 122.

[249] Hawking, *My Brief History*, 42.

[250] White/Gribbin, 132–133.

[251] Hawking, *Brief Answers*, 17.

[252] Levy, 93.

[253] Levy, 93.

[254] White/Gribbin, 161.

[255] Hawking, *My Brief History*, 6.
[256] White/Gribbin, 203.
[257] White/Gribbin, 204.
[258] White/Gribbin, 206.
[259] Hawking, *My Brief History*, 92.
[260] Hawking, *My Brief History*, 93.
[261] White/Gribbin, 223.
[262] White/Gribbin, 227.
[263] Hawking, *My Brief History*, 93.
[264] White/Gribbin, 240.
[265] Hawking, *My Brief History*, 97.
[266] Hawking, *My Brief History*, 97–98.
[267] Hawking, *My Brief History*, 98.
[268] Hawking, *My Brief History*, 99.
[269] Hawking, *My Brief History*, 99.
[270] Peter Guzzardi, quoted in White/Gribbin, 243.
[271] Hawking, *My Brief History*, 99.
[272] White/Gribbin, 244.
[273] White/Gribbin, 245.
[274] Hawking, quoted in White/Gribbin, 245.
[275] Levy, 136.
[276] White/Gribbin, 250.
[277] Hawking, *Brief Answers*, 81.
[278] Hawking, *Brief Answers*, 147.
[279] Levy, 123.
[280] Hawking, *Brief Answers*, 141.
[281] Hawking, *My Brief History*, 98.
[282] Levy, 115.
[283] Levy, 106–107.
[284] Levy, 6.

Chapter 5

[285] *Time*, quoted in Eig, 101.
[286] Eig, 301.
[287] Eig, 300.
[288] Eig, 98.
[289] Eig, 59.
[290] Hauser, 22.
[291] Hauser, 143–144.

[292] Eig, 519.
[293] Ali, quoted in Eig, 34.
[294] Eig, 100.
[295] Eig, 99.
[296] Ali, quoted in Hauser, 41.
[297] Neil Leifer, quoted in Hauser, 284.
[298] Dick Schaap, quoted in Hauser, 40.
[299] Mike Katz, quoted in Hauser, 290.
[300] Ed Schuyler, quoted in Hauser, 290–291.
[301] Eig, 80.
[302] Eig, 69.
[303] Eig, 104.
[304] Eig, 131.
[305] Hauser, 59–60.
[306] Eig, 39.
[307] Eig, 84–85.
[308] Ali, quoted in Hauser, 54–55.
[309] Ali, quoted in Hauser, 58.
[310] Mort Sharnik, quoted in Hauser, 70–71.
[311] Ali, quoted in Eig, 102.
[312] Eig, 141.
[313] From Ali's LP, *I'm The Greatest*, quoted in Hauser, 56.
[314] Izenberg, quoted in Hauser, 123.
[315] Eig, 115.
[316] Wilfred Sheed, quoted in Hauser, 291.
[317] Ali, quoted in Eig, 83.
[318] Eig, 107.
[319] Eig, 114.
[320] Ali, quoted in Eig, 153.
[321] Eig, 203.
[322] Martin Luther King Jr., quoted in Eig, 159.
[323] Eig, 258.
[324] Hauser, 102.
[325] Eig, 189.
[326] Ali, quoted in Hauser, 155.
[327] Arthur Daley, quoted in Hauser, 147.
[328] Eig, 240–241.
[329] Eig, 293.
[330] Elijah Muhammad, quoted in Hauser, 194.
[331] Jim Jacobs, quoted in Hauser, 209.

[332] Jim Jacobs, quoted in Hauser, 209.

[333] Eig, 308.

[334] Eig, 308.

[335] Dave Wolf, quoted in Hauser, 219.

[336] Joe Frazier, quoted in Hauser, 231.

[337] Eig, 383.

[338] See page 118 of this book.

[339] Ali, quoted in Eig, 381.

[340] Gene Kilroy, quoted in Eig, 264.

[341] Eig, 309.

[342] Eig, 328.

[343] Jim Brown, quoted in Eig, 365.

[344] Ali, quoted in Eig, 374.

[345] Eig, 374.

[346] Eig, 503.

[347] Eig, 530.

[348] Ali, quoted in Eig, 514.

Chapter 6

[349] Kranish/Fisher, vii.

[350] Kranish/Fisher, 3.

[351] D'Antonio, 17–18.

[352] D'Antonio, 12.

[353] D'Antonio, 3.

[354] D'Antonio, 3.

[355] Harold Seneker, quoted in Kranish/Fisher, 295.

[356] Quoted in D'Antonio, 313.

[357] Kranish/Fisher, 303.

[358] D'Antonio, 12.

[359] Kranish/Fisher, 111.

[360] Kranish/Fisher, 119

[361] Kranish/Fisher, 120.

[362] Trump/Zanker, 271.

[363] Trump/Zanker, 270.

[364] Trump, quoted in Kranish/Fisher, 104.

[365] Trump, quoted in Kranish/Fisher, 105.

[366] D'Antonio, 270.

[367] D'Antonio, 427.

[368] Kranish/Fisher, 132.

[369] George Rush, quoted in Kranish/Fisher, 110.

[370] Kranish/Fisher, 99.

[371] D'Antonio, 431–432.

[372] Trump quoted in Kranish/Fisher, 190.

[373] Trump quoted in D'Antonio, 220.

[374] Kranish/Fisher, 190.

[375] Kranish/Fisher, 228–229.

[376] Kranish/Fisher, 242.

[377] Trump during his presidential announcement speech, June 16, 2015.

[378] Trump during the October 19, 2016 presidential debate with Hillary Clinton.

[379] Trump on CNN, July 16, 2016.

[380] Trump during a Fox News interview, June 2015.

[381] Trump at a campaign rally in Fort Dodge, Iowa, November 12, 2015.

[382] Trump at a campaign rally in Portland, Maine, March 3, 2016.

[383] Trump on Twitter, January 9, 2016.

[384] Trump at a campaign rally in Atlanta, Georgia, June 15, 2016.

[385] Trump in an interview with Associated Press, May 13, 2016.

[386] Trump on Twitter, May 9, 2013.

[387] Trump, quoted in D'Antonio, 200.

[388] Trump on Fox & Friends, May 19, 2011.

[389] Trump, quoted in Kranish/Fisher, 105.

[390] Kranish/Fisher, 106.

[391] Trump/Zanker, 122.

[392] Trump/Zanker, 42.

[393] Trump/Zanker, 228.

[394] Trump/Zanker, 212.

[395] Trump, quoted in Kranish/Fisher, 42.

[396] D'Antonio, 61.

[397] Kranish/Fisher, 99.

[398] Trump, quoted in Kranish/Fisher, 213.

[399] D'Antonio, 16.

[400] Kranish/Fisher, 218.

[401] Kranish/Fisher, 224.

[402] Kranish/Fisher, 260.

[403] Kranish/Fisher, 290.

[404] D'Antonio, 291.

[405] D'Antonio, 320.

[406] D'Antonio, 440.

[407] D'Antonio, 442.

Chapter 7

[408] Andrews, 205.

[409] Schwarzenegger, *Total Recall*, 604.

[410] Hujer, 23.

[411] Schwarzenegger, quoted in Andrews, 18.

[412] Schwarzenegger, quoted in Andrews, 18.

[413] Schwarzenegger, *Total Recall*, 341–342.

[414] Schwarzenegger, *Total Recall*, 342.

[415] Schwarzenegger, *Total Recall*, 15–16.

[416] Schwarzenegger, *Education*, 19.

[417] Schwarzenegger, *Total Recall*, 31.

[418] Schwarzenegger, *Total Recall*, 68.

[419] Schwarzenegger, *Total Recall*, 102–103.

[420] Schwarzenegger, *Total Recall*, 69.

[421] Hujer, 47.

[422] Schwarzenegger, *Total Recall*, 152.

[423] Andrews, 64.

[424] Schwarzenegger, *Total Recall*, 153–154.

[425] Schwarzenegger, *Total Recall*, 159.

[426] Schwarzenegger, *Total Recall*, 162.

[427] Lommel, 13.

[428] Schwarzenegger, *Total Recall*, 163.

[429] Schwarzenegger, *Total Recall*, 176.

[430] Andrews, 57.

[431] Andrews, 37.

[432] Hujer, 105.

[433] Schwarzenegger, quoted in Andrews, 61.

[434] Schwarzenegger, quoted in Andrews, 74.

[435] Schwarzenegger, *Total Recall*, 204.

[436] Schwarzenegger, *Total Recall*, 204.

[437] Schwarzenegger, *Total Recall*, 213–214.

[438] Schwarzenegger, *Total Recall*, 227.

[439] Schwarzenegger, quoted in Andrews, 72–73.

[440] Schwarzenegger, quoted in Andrews, 72.

[441] Schwarzenegger, quoted in Goldstein.

[442] Schwarzenegger, *Total Recall*, 264.

[443] Schwarzenegger, *Total Recall*, 314.

[444] Schwarzenegger, *Total Recall*, 290.

[445] Schwarzenegger, *Total Recall*, 278.

[446] Schwarzenegger, *Total Recall*, 279.
[447] Schwarzenegger, *Total Recall*, 338.
[448] Schwarzenegger, *Total Recall*, 279.
[449] Schwarzenegger, *Total Recall*, 279.
[450] Schwarzenegger, *Total Recall*, 338.
[451] Schwarzenegger, *Total Recall*, 340.
[452] Schwarzenegger, *Total Recall*, 360.
[453] Schwarzenegger, quoted in Andrews, 155–156.
[454] Schwarzenegger, *Total Recall*, 374.
[455] Schwarzenegger, *Total Recall*, 389.
[456] Schwarzenegger, *Total Recall*, 388.
[457] Schwarzenegger, *Total Recall*, 388.
[458] Schwarzenegger, *Total Recall*, 390.
[459] Schwarzenegger, *Total Recall*, 459.
[460] Schwarzenegger, quoted in Hujer, 174.
[461] Schwarzenegger, *Total Recall*, 487.
[462] Schwarzenegger, *Total Recall*, 502.
[463] Schwarzenegger, *Total Recall*, 504.
[464] Schwarzenegger, *Total Recall*, 509–510.
[465] Schwarzenegger, *Total Recall*, 511.
[466] Schwarzenegger, *Total Recall*, 512.
[467] Schwarzenegger, *Total Recall*, 507.
[468] Schwarzenegger, *Total Recall*, 606.
[469] Schwarzenegger, quoted in *Cigar Aficianado* (https://www.cigaraficionado.com/article/the-world-according-to-arnold-6026).
[470] Schwarzenegger, quoted in Hujer, 27.
[471] Schwarzenegger, *Total Recall*, 618.

Chapter 8

[472] Quoted in Kelley, 274.
[473] Kelley, 348.
[474] Kelley, 18 et seq.
[475] Kelley, 44.
[476] Kelley, 43–44, 66.
[477] Winfrey, quoted in Kelley, 162.
[478] Kelley, 46.
[479] Kelley, 52.
[480] Kelley, 69.
[481] Kelley, 79.

[482] Bob Turk, quoted in Kelley, 81.

[483] Kelley, 81.

[484] Kelley, 83.

[485] Kelley, 83.

[486] Bill Baker, quoted in Kelley, 91.

[487] Kelley, 92.

[488] Winfrey, quoted in Kelley, 94.

[489] Kelley, 95.

[490] Kelley, 96.

[491] Clarence Petersen, quoted in Kelley, 116.

[492] Winfrey, quoted in Kelley, 117.

[493] Kelley, 130.

[494] Kelley, 134.

[495] Kelley, 2.

[496] Kelley, 161.

[497] Kelley, 139.

[498] Kelley, 158–159.

[499] Kelley, 97.

[500] Kelley, 11–13.

[501] Kelley, 6.

[502] Kelley, 7.

[503] Kelley, 6.

[504] Kelley, 193–194.

[505] Kelley, 5.

[506] Kelley, 34–35.

[507] Kelley, 182.

[508] Andy Behrman, quoted in Kelley, 182.

[509] Chicago Tribune, cited in Kelley, 112.

[510] Kelley, 197.

[511] Kelley, 241–243.

[512] Phil Donahue, quoted in Kelley, 197.

[513] Winfrey, quoted in Kelley, 239.

[514] Kelley, 239.

[515] Winfrey, quoted in Kelley, 260.

[516] Winfrey, quoted in Kelley, 334.

[517] Winfrey, quoted in Kelley, 337.

[518] Winfrey, quoted in Kelley, 270.

[519] Peck, 12.

[520] Winfrey, quoted in Kelley, 223.

[521] Winfrey, quoted in Peck, 8.

[522] Winfrey, quoted in Peck, 9.

[523] Winfrey quoted in George/McLean, 4.

[524] Crosby, 47.

[525] Crosby, 114.

[526] Crosby, 74.

[527] Winfrey quoted in Crosby, 104.

[528] Kelley, 224.

[529] Kelley, 347.

[530] Kelley, 345.

[531] Kelley, 329.

[532] Stedman Graham, quoted in Kelley, 330.

[533] Winfrey, quoted in Kelley, 227.

[534] Kelley, 228.

[535] Kelley, 227.

[536] Kelley, 228.

[537] Kelley, 280.

[538] Kelley, 274.

[539] http://www.oprah.com/entertainment/the-oprah-winfrey-show-by-the-numbers-oprah-show-statistics/all

[540] Peck, 10.

[541] Kelley, 189.

[542] Crosby, 14.

[543] Kelley, 123.

[544] Kelley, 329.

[545] Whoopi Goldberg, quoted in Kelley, 333.

[546] Jonathan Demme, quoted in Kelley, 333.

[547] Kelley, 383.

[548] Kelley, 380.

[549] Kelley, 379.

Chapter 9

[550] Hertzfeld, quoted in Isaacson, *Jobs*, 109.

[551] Schlender/Tetzeli, 25.

[552] Schlender/Tetzeli, 44.

[553] Jobs, quoted in Isaacson, *Jobs*, 132.

[554] Bill Gates, quoted in Isaacson, *Jobs*, 161.

[555] Hawkins, quoted in Gallo, *Innovation Secrets*, 58.

[556] Alvey Ray Smith, quoted in Isaacson, *Jobs*, 220.

[557] Alvey Ray Smith, quoted in Isaacson, *Jobs*, 224.

[558] Jobs, quoted in Isaacson, *Jobs*, 141.
[559] Jobs, quoted in Isaacson, *Jobs*, 143.
[560] Jobs, quoted in Isaacson, *Jobs*, 85.
[561] Trip Hawkins quoting Steve Jobs in Gallo, *Innovation Secrets*, 59.
[562] Jobs, quoted in Isaacson, *Jobs*, 296.
[563] Gallo, *Innovation Secrets*, 6.
[564] Isaacson, *Jobs*, 326.
[565] Isaacson, *Jobs*, 338.
[566] Isaacson, *Jobs*, 149.
[567] Jobs, quoted in Isaacson, *Jobs*, 155.
[568] Isaacson, *Jobs*, 124–125.
[569] Gallo, *Presentation Secrets*, 2.
[570] Gallo, *Presentation Secrets*, 75.
[571] Isaacson, *Jobs*, 132.
[572] Ive, quoted in Isaacson, *Jobs*, 320.
[573] Schlender/Tetzeli, 53.
[574] Schlender/Tetzeli, 228.
[575] *Time*, quoted in Isaacson, *Jobs*, 128.
[576] Jobs, quoted in Isaacson, *Jobs*, 129.
[577] Isaacson, *Jobs*, 129.
[578] Cook, quoted in Isaacson, *Jobs*, 422–423.
[579] Isaacson, *Jobs*, 281.
[580] Jobs, quoted in Young/Simon, 65.
[581] Michael Dell, quoted in Schlender/Tetzeli, 215.
[582] Schlender/Tetzeli, 221.
[583] Jobs, quoted in Gallo, *Innovation Secrets*, 109.
[584] Quoted in Isaacson, *Jobs*, 303.
[585] Schlender/Tetzeli, 100.
[586] Hertzfeld, quoted in Isaacson, *Jobs*, 113.
[587] Isaacson, *Jobs*, 113.
[588] Isaacson, *Jobs*, 116.
[589] Jobs, quoted in Isaacson, *Jobs*, 123.
[590] Atkinson, quoted in Isaacson, *Jobs*, 123.
[591] Jobs, quoted in Isaacson, *Jobs*, 316.
[592] Jobs, quoted in Isaacson, *Jobs*, 523.
[593] Jobs, quoted in Isaacson, *Jobs*, 31.
[594] Isaacson, *Jobs*, 34–35.
[595] Isaacson, *Jobs*, 28.
[596] Jobs, quoted in Isaacson, *Jobs*, 112.
[597] Isaacson, *Jobs*, 333.

[598] Isaacson, *Jobs*, 214.

[599] Isaacson, *Jobs*, 214.

[600] Isaacson, *Jobs*, 151–152.

[601] Isaacson, *Jobs*, 216.

[602] Schlender/Tetzeli, 161.

[603] Schlender/Tetzeli, 9.

[604] Schlender/Tetzeli, 100.

[605] Gallo, *Presentation Secrets*, 39.

[606] Gallo, *Presentation Secrets*, 42.

[607] Schlender/Tetzeli, 259.

[608] Schumpeter, 118.

[609] Schumpeter, 119.

[610] Schumpeter, 120.

[611] Schumpeter, 121.

[612] Schumpeter, 128.

[613] Schumpeter, 132.

[614] Schumpeter, 152.

[615] Schumpeter, 163–164.

Chapter 10

[616] https://www.billboard.com/charts/greatest-hot-100-artists

[617] http://content.time.com/time/specials/packages/
article/0,28804,2029774_2029776_2031853,00.html

[618] Taraborrelli, 447.

[619] Taraborrelli, 479.

[620] Camille Barbone, quoted in O'Brien, 45–46.

[621] Anthony Jackson, quoted in O'Brien, 64.

[622] O'Brien, 213.

[623] Taraborrelli, 257.

[624] Taraborrelli, 258.

[625] O'Brien, 214, Taraborrelli, 258.

[626] Taraborrelli, 69.

[627] Madonna, quoted in Taraborrelli, 8.

[628] Madonna, quoted in Taraborrelli, 110.

[629] Taraborrelli, 8.

[630] O'Brien, 107.

[631] Taraborrelli, 36.

[632] Erica Bell recalls a conversation with Madonna, quoted in Taraborrelli, 79.

[633] Madonna, quoted in Taraborrelli, 9.

[634] Madonna, quoted in Taraborrelli, 125.

[635] Madonna, quoted in O'Brien, 32.

[636] O'Brien, 32.

[637] O'Brien, 38.

[638] Madonna, quoted in Taraborrelli, 47.

[639] Johnny Dynell, quoted in O'Brien, 76.

[640] Madonna, quoted in O'Brien, 78.

[641] Madonna, quoted in Taraborrelli, 28.

[642] Madonna, quoted in Taraborrelli, 28.

[643] Madonna, quoted in Taraborrelli, 36.

[644] Madonna, quoted in O'Brien, x.

[645] Taraborrelli, 97.

[646] O'Brien, 134.

[647] O'Brien, 81.

[648] O'Brien, 151.

[649] O'Brien, 151.

[650] O'Brien, 163–164.

[651] *The Washington Post*, quoted in Taraborrelli, 233.

[652] *The Observer*, quoted in O'Brien, 171.

[653] Taraborrelli, 233.

[654] O'Brien, 171.

[655] Taraborrelli, 237.

[656] Taraborrelli, 237.

[657] O'Brien, 193.

[658] O'Brien, 193.

[659] Taraborrelli, 240.

[660] O'Brien, 198.

[661] O'Brien, 198.

[662] O'Brien, 199.

[663] Madonna, quoted in Taraborrelli, 246–247.

[664] Anonymous member of Madonna's management team, quoted in Taraborrelli, 247.

[665] Taraborrelli, 252.

[666] Taraborrelli, 254.

[667] Taraborrelli, 286.

[668] O'Brien, 217.

[669] Taraborrelli, 302.

[670] Taraborrelli, 303.

[671] Jimmy Bralower, quoted in O'Brien, 75.

[672] Quoted in O'Brien, 91.

[673] Taraborrelli, 125, 134, 341.
[674] Taraborrelli, 420, 431.
[675] Taraborrelli, 125–126.
[676] Sean Penn, quoted in Taraborrelli, 137.
[677] Madonna, quoted in Taraborrelli, 137.
[678] Taraborrelli, 138.
[679] Taraborrelli, 226.
[680] O'Brien, 189.
[681] Madonna, quoted in St. Michael, 95.
[682] https://womeninmusic.voices.wooster.edu/wp-content/uploads/sites/123/2017/12/Paglia-Madonna-Finally-a-Real-Feminist.pdf
[683] Camille Paglia, quoted in Taraborrelli, 479.
[684] https://www.stern.de/lifestyle/leute/madonna--ihr-neuer-freund-ist-taenzer-und-36-jahre-juenger-als-sie-9051276.html
[685] Madonna, quoted in Norton, 46.

Chapter 11

[686] Ruth Rudge, quoted in Brown, 64.
[687] Brown, 71.
[688] Brown, 71.
[689] Paul Johnson, quoted in Brown, 71.
[690] Brown, 62.
[691] Diana, quoted in Brown, 63.
[692] *Tatler*, quoted in Brown, 152.
[693] Brown, 210.
[694] Quoted in Brown, 210.
[695] Brown, 278.
[696] Brown, 29.
[697] Diana, quoted in Brown, 30.
[698] Barbara Cartland, quoted in Brown, 89.
[699] Brown, 261.
[700] Brown, 153.
[701] Brown, 154.
[702] Brown, 21.
[703] Brown, 22.
[704] Brown, 152.
[705] Brown, 153.
[706] Ashley Walton, quoted in Brown, 240.
[707] Brown, 455.

[708] Quoted in Brown, 456.

[709] Brown, 456.

[710] Brown, 392.

[711] Diana, quoted in Brown, 379.

[712] Brown, 380.

[713] Brown, 420.

[714] Prince Charles, quoted in Brown, 381.

[715] Prince Charles, quoted in Brown, 382.

[716] Brown, 280.

[717] Brown, 417.

[718] Brown, 417.

[719] Brown, 466.

[720] Diana, quoted in Brown, 473.

[721] Diana, quoted in Brown, 468.

[722] Diana, quoted in Brown, 473.

[723] Brown, 475.

[724] Vivienne Parry, quoted in Brown, 440.

[725] Brown, 341.

[726] Brown, 441.

[727] Brown, 331.

[728] Brown, 73.

[729] Brown, 74.

[730] Diana, quoted in Brown, 74.

[731] Brown, 258.

[732] Frances Shand Kydd, quoted in Brown, 258.

[733] Quoted in Brown, 332–333.

[734] Brown, 332.

[735] Christiana Lamb, *Sunday Times*, quoted in Brown, 14.

[736] Vivienne Parry, quoted in Brown, 396.

[737] Judy Wade, quoted in Brown, 224–225.

[738] Brown, 260–261.

[739] Ashley Walton, quoted in Brown, 261.

[740] Brown, 435.

[741] Patricia Dreyer, foreword to the German edition of Brown's biography, XIV–XV.

[742] Brown, 511.

Chapter 12

[743] As of 31 July 2021

[744] https://www.harpersbazaar.com/celebrity/latest/a22117965/kardashian-family-net-worth/

[745] Kim Kardashian, quoted in Smith, 52.

[746] Smith, 99.

[747] Smith, 106.

[748] Smith, 105.

[749] Smith, 113.

[750] Smith, 114.

[751] Smith, 112.

[752] Sastre, 125.

[753] Oppenheimer, 245.

[754] Smith, 120.

[755] Smith, 125.

[756] Smith, 270.

[757] Smith, 128.

[758] Figures from July 2021.

[759] Smith, 270.

[760] Kim, quoted in Smith, 146.

[761] Smith, 147.

[762] *The Observer*, quoted in Smith, 148.

[763] Smith, 148.

[764] Smith, 150.

[765] Smith, 153.

[766] Kim, quoted in Smith, 153.

[767] Damon Thomas, quoted in Oppenheimer, 250.

[768] Kourtney Kardashian, quoted in Smith, 155.

[769] Kim, quoted in Smith, 155.

[770] Smith, 156.

[771] Kim, quoted in Smith, 156.

[772] Smith, 157.

[773] Smith, 158.

[774] Smith, 158.

[775] Smith, 272.

[776] Smith, 158.

[777] Smith, 273.

[778] Sastre, 132.

[779] https://www.telegraph.co.uk/fashion/people/the-man-behind-kim-kardashians-paper-magazine-cover-on-how-to-br/

[780] Mickey Boardman, quoted in Oppenheimer, 270.

[781] Mickey Boardman, quoted in Oppenheimer, 265.

[782] Klazas, 20.

[783] Smith, 272.

[784] Smith, 202.

[785] Smith, 187.

[786] Smith, 275.

[787] Harvey, 653.

[788] Harvey, 656–657.

[789] Smith, 232.

[790] Smith, 276,

[791] https://www.forbes.com/sites/natalierobehmed/2018/07/11/why-kim-kardashian-west-is-worth-350-million/#5c3a1104f7b6

[792] https://www.nytimes.com/2019/03/30/style/kardashians-interview.html

[793] Boileau, 5.

[794] Smith, 247.

[795] Oppenheimer, 257.

[796] https://www.denverpost.com/2011/12/15/people-you-dont-have-talent-barbara-walters-tells-kardashians/

[797] Alice Leppert, quoted in Klazas, 19.

[798] https://www.byrdie.com/kim-kardashian-career-tips-4775501

BIBLIOGRAPHY

Andrews, Nigel. *True Myths. The Life and Times of Arnold Schwarzenegger.* New York, N.Y.: Bloomsbury: 2003.

Beahm, George. *I, Steve: Steve Jobs in his own Words.* Chicago, Ill.: B2 Books: 2011.

Becker, Tobias, Ullrich Fichtner, Lothar Gorris, Alexander Kühn, Britta Sandberg, and Claudia Voigt. "Ich, Karl." *Der Spiegel,* No. 9, February 23, 2019.

Bockris, Victor. *Warhol: The Biography.* London: Frederick Muller: 1988.

Boileau, Brandon. "Constructing the Self in Selfish: a Journey into the Celebrification of Kim Kardashian West," Final Research Paper: CMCT 6135: May 9, 2017.

Brown, Tina. *The Diana Chronicles.* New York: Anchor Books: 2008.

Brown, Tina. *Diana. Die Biographie.* Munich: Droemer-Knaur Verlag: 2007.

Calaprice, Alice (ed.). *The Expanded Quotable Einstein.* Princeton, N.J.: Princeton University Press: 2000.

Crosby, Marianne Jeanette. "Viewing the World through Oprah's Eyes. A Framing Analysis of the Spiritual Views of Oprah Winfrey." Presented to the Faculty at Liberty University School of Communication in partial fulfilment of the requirements for the Master of Arts in Communication, May 2009.

D'Antonio, Michael. *The Truth About Trump.* New York, N.Y.: St Martin's Press: 2015.

Eig, Jonathan. *Ali. A Life.* London: Simon & Schuster: 2017.

Frank, Marcie. "Popping Off Warhol: From the Gutter to the Underground and Beyond" in Doyle, Jennifer, Jonathan Flatley and Jose Esteban Munoz (eds). *Pop Out: Queer Warhol.* Durham, NC and London: Duke University Press: 1996.

Gallo, Carmine. *The Presentation Secrets of Steve Jobs*. New York, N.Y.: McGraw Hill: 2010.

Gallo, Carmine. *The Innovation Secrets of Steve Jobs*. New York, N.Y.: McGraw Hill: 2011.

George, Bill & McLean, Andrew N. "Oprah!" *Harvard Business School*, 9-405-087, Rev: April 11, 2007.

Goldsmith, Kenneth (ed.). *I'll be Your Mirror. The Selected Andy Warhol Interviews 1962–1987*: New York, N.Y.: Carroll & Graf Publishers: 2004.

Goldstein, Patrick. "The Arnold Era" in *Los Angeles Times Magazine*. Los Angeles: June 16, 1996. Available at https://www.latimes.com/archives/la-xpm-1996-06-16-tm-15451-story.html (accessed on 05.22.2020.)

Graw, Ansgar. *Trump verrückt die Welt. Wie der US-Präsident sein Land und die Geopolitik verändert*. Stuttgart: Herbig-Verlag: 2017.

Harvey, Alison. "The Fame Game: Working Your Way Up the Celebrity Ladder" in *Kim Kardashian: Hollywood*, in: *Games and Culture 2018*, Vol. 13 (7), 652–670.

Hauser, Thomas. *Muhammad Ali: His Life and Times*. New York, N.Y.: Simon & Schuster: 1991.

Hawking, Stephen. *Brief Answers to the Big Questions*. London: John Murray: 2018.

Hawking, Stephen. *My Brief History*. New York, N.Y.: Bantam Books: 2013.

Hawking, Jane. *Travelling to Infinity: My Life with Stephen*. Richmond, UK: Alma Books: 2014.

Hujer, Marc. *Arnold Schwarzenegger. Die Biographie*. Munich: Deutsche Verlags-Anstalt: 2009.

Illy, József (ed.). *Albert Meets America. How Journalists Treated Genius During Einstein's 1921 Travels*. Baltimore, Maryland: The Johns Hopkins University Press: 2006.

Indiana, Gary & Warhol, Andy. *Andy Warhol and the Can that Sold the World*. New York, N.Y.: Basic Books: 2010.

Isaacson, Walter. *Steve Jobs*. London: Simon & Schuster: 2011.

Isaacson, Walter. *Einstein. His Life and Universe*. London, Sydney, New York, Toronto: Pocket Books: 2007.

Kelley, Kitty. *Oprah. A Biography*. New York, N.Y.: Crown Publishers: 2010.

Klazas, Erin B. "Selfhood, Citizenship … and All Things Kardashian: Neoliberal and Postfeminist Ideals in Reality Television." Ursinus College, Media and Communication Studies Summer Fellows: 2015.

Koestenbaum, Wayne. *Andy Warhol.* London: Weidenfeld & Nicolson: 2001.

Kranish, Michael & Fisher, Marc. *Trump Revealed: An American Journey of Ambition, Ego, Money, and Power.* New York, N.Y.: Scribner: 2016.

Leamer, Laurence. *Fantastic. The Life of Arnold Schwarzenegger.* London: Sidgwick & Jackson: 2005.

Levy, Joel. *Hawking: The Man, the Genius, and the Theory of Everything.* London: André Deutsch: 2018.

Lommel, Cookie. *Schwarzenegger. A Man with a Plan.* Munich: Wilhelm Heyne Verlag: 2004.

Maillard, Arnaud. *Karl Lagerfeld und ich. 15 Jahre an der Seite des Modezaren.* Munich: Wilhelm Heyne Verlag: 2009.

Neffe, Jürgen. *Einstein. A Biography. Translated by Shelley Frisch:* New York, N.Y.: Farrar, Straus and Giroux: 2007.

Norton, Kelley Robyn. "Personal Branding im Musikbusiness," bachelor's thesis, Hochschule Mittweida: 2014.

Oppenheimer, Jerry. *The Kardashians. An American Dream.* New York, N.Y.: St. Martin's Press: 2017.

O'Brien, Lucy. *Madonna. Like an Icon.* New York, N.Y.: HarperEntertainment: 2007.

Parsons, Paul & Dixon, Gail. *3-Minute Stephen Hawking: His Life, Theories and Influence in 3-Minute Particles.* New York, N.Y.: Metro Books. 2012.

Peck, Janice. "The Secret of Her Success: Oprah Winfrey and the Seductions of Self-Transformation," in *Journal of Communication Inquiry* 34 (1), 7–14.

Sahner, Paul. *Karl. Mit Ergänzungskapiteln von Katharina Pfannkuch.* Munich: mvg Verlag: 2009.

Sastre, Alexandra. "Hottentot in the age of reality TV: Sexuality, race, and Kim Kardashian's visible body," in *Celebrity Studies,* 2014, Vol. 5, Nos. 1-2, 123–137.

Schlender, Brent & Tetzell, Rick. *Becoming Steve Jobs. How a Reckless Upstart Became a Visionary Leader.* London: Sceptre: 2015.

Schumpeter, Joseph. *Theorie der wirtschaftlichen Entwicklung*. Leipzig: Duncker & Humblot: 2012.

Schwarzenegger, Arnold & Hall, Douglas Kent. *Arnold: The Education of a Bodybuilder*. New York, N.Y.: Simon & Schuster: 1993.

Schwarzenegger, Arnold, with Petre, Peter. *Total Recall. My Unbelievably True Life Story*. London: Simon & Schuster: 2012.

Skiena, Steven & Ward, Charles B. *Who's Bigger? Where Historical Figures Really Rank*. New York, N.Y.: Cambridge University Press: 2014.

Smith, Sean. *Kim*. New York, N.Y.: Dey St.: 2015.

Spohn, Annette. *Andy Warhol*. Frankfurt am Main: Suhrkamp Verlag: 2008.

St. Michael, Mick. *Madonna In Her Own Words*. London / New York / Sydney: Omnibus Press: 1990.

Taraborrelli, J. Randy. *Madonna. An Intimate Biography of an Icon at Sixty. Updated edition*. London: Sidgwick & Jackson: 2018.

Trump, Donald & Zanker, Bill. *Think Big and Kick Ass in Business and in Life*. New York, N.Y.: Collins: 2007.

Warhol, Andy & Hackett, Pat. *POPism: The Warhol Sixties*. New York, N.Y.: Houghtom Mifflin Harcourt Publishing Company: 1980.

White, Michael & Gribbin, John. *Stephen Hawking. A Life in Science*. New York, N.Y.: Dutton; 1992.

Young, Jeffrey S. & Simon, William L. *iCon: Steve Jobs, The Greatest Second Act in the History of Business*. Hoboken, New Jersey: John Wiley & Sons: 2005.

INDEX OF PERSONS